Noh

FORMS OF DRAMA

Forms of Drama meets the need for accessible, mid-length volumes that offer undergraduate readers authoritative guides to the distinct forms of global drama. From classical Greek tragedy to Chinese pear garden theatre, cabaret to *kathakali*, the series equips readers with models and methodologies for analysing a wide range of performance practices and engaging with these as "craft".

SERIES EDITOR: SIMON SHEPHERD

Badhai: Hijra-Khwaja Sira-Trans *Performance across Borders in South Asia*
978-1-3501-7453-5
Adnan Hossain, Claire Pamment and Jeff Roy

Cabaret
978-1-3501-4025-7
William Grange

Classical Greek Tragedy
978-1-3501-4456-9
Judith Fletcher

The Commedia dell'Arte
978-1-3501-4418-7
Domenico Pietropaolo

Documentary Theatre and Performance
Andy Lavender
978-1-3501-3713-4

Kathakali: Tradition, Innovations, and Transitions in the Dance Drama of Kerala
Sudha Gopalakrishnan
978-1-3502-3632-5

Kaṭṭaikkūttu: A Rural Theatre Tradition in South India
978-1-3502-3660-8
Hanne M. de Bruin

Korean Pansori as Voice Theatre: History, Theory, Practice
Chan E. Park
978-1-3501-7488-7

Liyuanxi – Chinese "Pear Garden Theatre"
978-1-3501-5739-2
Josh Stenberg

Modern Tragedy
978-1-3501-3977-0
James Moran

Nautanki: The Musical Theatre of North India
Devendra Sharma
978-1-3502-9672-5

Pageant
978-1-3501-4451-4
Joan FitzPatrick Dean

Romantic Comedy
978-1-3501-8337-7
Trevor R. Griffiths

Satire
978-1-3501-4007-3
Joel Schechter

Tragicomedy
978-1-3501-4430-9
Brean Hammond

Noh

Japanese Classical Dance-drama

Kaoru Nakao and Diego Pellecchia

methuen | drama
LONDON • NEW YORK • OXFORD • NEW DELHI • SYDNEY

METHUEN DRAMA
Bloomsbury Publishing Plc
50 Bedford Square, London, WC1B 3DP, UK
1385 Broadway, New York, NY 10018, USA
29 Earlsfort Terrace, Dublin 2, Ireland

BLOOMSBURY, METHUEN DRAMA and the Methuen Drama logo are trademarks of Bloomsbury Publishing Plc

First published in Great Britain 2025

For legal purposes the Acknowledgments on p. xviii constitute an extension of this copyright page.

Series design by Charlotte Daniels

A catalogue record for this book is available from the British Library.

A catalog record for this book is available from the Library of Congress.

ISBN: HB: 978-1-3503-7144-6
ePDF: 978-1-3503-7146-0
eBook: 978-1-3503-7145-3

Series: Forms of Drama

Typeset by Integra Software Services Pvt. Ltd.

I am grateful, as always, to Mick Wallis for helping me to think through these issues. Any clumsiness or stupidity is entirely my own.

Simon Shepherd

CONTENTS

FIGURES

SERIES PREFACE

The scope of this series is scripted aesthetic activity that works by means of personation.

Scripting is done in a wide variety of ways. It may, most obviously, be the more or less detailed written text familiar in the stage play of the Western tradition, which not only provides lines to be spoken but directions for speaking them. Or it may be a set of instructions, a structure or scenario, on the basis of which performers improvise, drawing, as they do so, on an already learnt repertoire of routines and responses. Or there may be nothing written, just sets of rules, arrangements and even speeches orally handed down over time. The effectiveness of such unwritten scripting can be seen in the behaviour of audiences, who, without reading a script, have learnt how to conduct themselves appropriately at the different activities they attend. For one of the key things that unwritten script specifies and assumes is the relationship between the various groups of participants, including the separation, or not, between doers and watchers.

What is scripted is specifically an aesthetic activity. That specification distinguishes drama from non-aesthetic activity using personation. Following the work of Erving Goffman in the mid-1950s, especially his book *The Presentation of Self in Everyday Life*, the social sciences have made us richly aware of the various ways in which human interactions are performed. Going shopping, for example, is a performance in that we present a version of ourselves in each encounter we make. We may indeed have changed our clothes before setting out. This, though, is a social performance.

The distinction between social performance and aesthetic activity is not clear-cut. The two sorts of practice overlap and mingle with one another. An activity may be more or less aesthetic, but the crucial distinguishing feature is the status of the aesthetic element. Going shopping may contain an aesthetic element – decisions about clothes and shoes to wear – but its purpose is not deliberately to make an aesthetic activity or to mark itself as different from everyday social life. The aesthetic element is not regarded as a general requirement. By contrast a courtroom trial may be seen as a social performance, in that it has an important social function, but it is at the same time extensively scripted, with prepared speeches, costumes and choreography. This scripted aesthetic element assists the social function in that it conveys a sense of more than everyday importance and authority to proceedings which can have life-changing impact. Unlike the activity of going shopping, the aesthetic element here is not optional. Derived from tradition, it is a required component that gives the specific identity to the activity.

It is defined as an activity in that, in a way different from a painting of Rembrandt's mother or a statue of Ramesses II, something is made to happen over time. And, unlike a symphony concert or firework display, that activity works by means of personation. Such personation may be done by imitating and interpreting – "inhabiting" – other human beings, fictional or historical, and it may use the bodies of human performers or puppets. But it may also be done by a performer who produces a version of their own self, such as a stand-up comedian or court official on duty, or by a performer who, through doing the event, acquires a self with special status, as with the *hijras* securing their sacredness by doing the ritual practice of *badhai*.

Some people prefer to call many of these sorts of scripted aesthetic events not drama but cultural performance. But there are problems with this. First, such labeling tends to keep in place an old-fashioned idea of Western scholarship that drama, with its origins in ancient Greece, is a specifically European "high" art. Everything outside it is then potentially, and damagingly, consigned to a domain which may be neither "art" nor "high". Instead the European stage play and its like can best be regarded as a subset of the general category, distinct from the rest in that two groups of people come together in order specifically to present and watch a story being acted out by imitating other persons and settings. Thus the performance of a stage play in this tradition consists of two levels of activity using personation: the interaction of audience and performers and the interaction between characters in a fictional story.

The second problem with the category of cultural performance is that it downplays the significance and persistence of script, in all its varieties. With its roots in the traditional behaviours and beliefs of a society, script gives specific instructions for the form – the materials, the structure and sequence – of the aesthetic activity, the drama. And as we have noted, script also defines the relationships between those who are present in different capacities at the event.

It is only by attending to what is scripted, to the form of the drama, that we can best analyse its functions and pleasures. At its most simple, analysis of form enables us to distinguish between different sorts of aesthetic activity. The masks used in *kathakali* look different from those used in *commedia dell'arte*. They are made of different materials, designs and colours. The roots of those differences lie in their separate cultural traditions and systems of living. For similar reasons the puppets of *karagoz* and *wayang* differ. But perhaps more importantly the attention to form provides a basis for exploring the operation and effects of a particular work. Those who regularly participate in and watch drama, of whatever sort, learn to recognise and remember the forms of what they see and hear. When one drama has family resemblances to another, in its organisation and use of materials, structure and sequences, those who attend it develop expectations as to how it will – or indeed should – operate. It then becomes possible to specify how a particular work subverts, challenges or enhances these expectations.

Expectation doesn't only govern response to individual works, however. It can shape, indeed has shaped, assumptions about which dramas are worth studying. It is well established that Asia has ancient and rich dramatic traditions, from the Indian sub-continent to Japan, as does Europe, and these are studied with enthusiasm. But there is much less widespread activity, at least in Western universities, in relation to the traditions of, say, Africa, Latin America and the Middle East. Secondly, even within the recognised traditions, there are assumptions that some dramas are more "artistic," or indeed more "serious," "higher" even, than others. Thus it may be assumed that nō or classical tragedy will require the sort of close attention to craft which is not necessary for mumming or *badhai*.

Both sets of assumptions here keep in place a system which allocates value. This series aims to counteract a discriminatory value system by ranging as widely as possible across world practices and by giving the same sort of attention to all the forms it features. Thus book-length studies of forms such as *al-halqa*, *hana keaka* and *ta'zieh* will appear in English for perhaps the first time. Those studies, just like those of *kathakali*, tragicomedy and the rest, will adopt the same basic approach. That approach consists of an historical overview of the development of a form combined with, indeed anchored in, detailed analysis of examples and case studies. One of the benefits of properly detailed analysis is that it can reveal the construction which gives a work the appearance of being serious, artistic, and indeed "high".

What does that work of construction is script. This series is grounded in the idea that all forms of drama have script of some kind and that an understanding of drama, of any sort, has to include analysis of that script. In taking this approach, books in this series again challenge an assumption which has in recent times governed the study of drama. Deriving from the supposed, but artificial, distinction between cultural performance and drama, many accounts of cultural performance ignore its scriptedness and assume that the proper way of studying it is simply to describe how its practitioners behave and what they make. This is useful enough, but to leave it at that is to produce something that looks like a form of lesser anthropology. The description of behaviours is only the first step in that it establishes what the script is. The next step is to analyse how the script and form work and how they create effect.

But it goes further than this. The close-up analyses of materials, structures and sequences – of scripted forms – show how they emerge from and connect deeply back into the modes of life and belief to which they are necessary. They tell us in short why, in any culture, the drama needs to be done. Thus by adopting the extended model of drama, and by approaching all dramas in the same way, the books in this series aim to tell us why, in all societies, the activities of scripted aesthetic personation – dramas – keep happening, and need to keep happening.

ACKNOWLEDGMENTS

Our understanding of nō is enriched by a myriad of connections in both the study and practice of this art. It is simply impossible to list all the people to whom we are indebted. We would like to thank the following people for providing us with photographic material that was essential for illustrating and analyzing the contents of this book: Kongō School actors Kongō Tatsunori and Teshima Kōji; Hōshō School actors Tatsumi Manjirō and Waku Sōtarō; playwright Izumi Noriko; Nō mask makers Miichi Yasuo and Fujiwara Chisa; photographers Halca Uesugi and Fabio Massimo Fioravanti; and the Noh Theatre Research Institute of Hōsei University. We are grateful to Udaka Tatsushige and Rebecca Teele Ogamo for their assistance with technical aspects of performance and mask making, and to the students who participated in our online and face-to-face classes, which formed the basis of our writing.

We are also grateful to Series Editor Simon Shepherd and Assistant Editor Ella Wilson. Books on nō are usually written for a specialized audience, and we appreciate the bold effort to include nō in this series, which introduces theatre forms from around the world. Finally, we would like to thank Jonah Salz for his support in the early stages of planning this book, and Jane Traynor for creating the index.

NOTE TO THE READER

As an introductory volume on nō, we have designed this book primarily for undergraduate students in theatre departments and Japanese studies departments, although we believe it may also be useful to postgraduate students, researchers, and practitioners seeking a compact yet comprehensive introduction to this art. Our goal was to use clear and accessible language to reach readers who may be unfamiliar with nō or Japanese performing arts. At the same time, we aimed to provide accuracy and depth to satisfy those with prior knowledge. We believe this approach will make the content widely accessible, while preserving the detail and precision required for academic discussion. For bibliographic references we have used English-language scholarship wherever possible, but we have also included Japanese sources when necessary. In either case, our list of references is by no means exhaustive; there is also an increasing amount of audiovisual material available online, which we encourage the reader to use as a supplement to this volume. We recommend some of them after the bibliography.

In order to suggest ways to analyze nō, we constantly refer to two masterpieces of the nō repertory: *Atsumori* and *Sumidagawa*, representatives of two styles of nō dramaturgy and stage presentations. For quotes from the plays we have used Royall Tyler's translations in *Japanese Nō Dramas* (Penguin Classics) because of their literary value and accessibility. Although in English nō is often referred to as being "theatre," in the title of this book we have chosen to use the expression "dance-drama" to emphasize the importance of choreographed movement in nō performance.

We follow a modified Hepburn system for romanizing Japanese terms, using macrons for all long vowels except place names and other common terms. In the title of the book we use "noh" rather than "nō" to facilitate the visualization and online accessibility of the volume, as not all typesets are able to reproduce the macron "ō." We italicize foreign words except those commonly used in English, such as shogun and kimono, as well as nō and kyōgen, which are frequently used in the book. Japanese people's names follow the conventional surname-first order.

As for the periodization of Japanese history, we follow this system:

Asuka (538–710)
Nara (710–793)
Heian (794–1185)
Kamakura (1185–1333)
Muromachi (1336–1573)
Momoyama (1573–1603)
Edo (1603–1868)
Meiji (1868–1912)
Taishō (1912–1926)
Shōwa (1926–1989)
Heisei (1989–2019)
Reiwa (2019–)

Introduction

In lectures, public speeches, or interviews, nō scholars often face the challenge of providing a comprehensive yet succinct introduction to this intricate art form. Navigating the complexity of nō is no small feat. In our book, we strive to offer an introduction that explores various facets of nō, including its historical context, the literary foundations of the plays, and the essential elements of performance—such as dance, music, masks, and costumes. Most importantly, we aim to emphasize the tight interplay of these components. In Japanese, nō is often referred to as *sōgō geijutsu* (integrated art), highlighting how its multiple elements can be considered individually but also in relation to each other, creating a complex and cohesive art form. Due to the inherent mutual relationship between these various components, listing them in a sequential order, as the book format requires, proves challenging. Nevertheless, we have made efforts to underscore their interconnectedness by using cross-references between chapters whenever possible.

The introduction gives a general outline of the main elements of nō before moving on to introduce two plays, *Atsumori* and *Sumidagawa*, which are recurrently quoted and analyzed throughout the book. These plays were chosen to represent the two main dramaturgical patterns of nō: *mugen* ("dream and illusion") and *genzai* ("present time"). First, we explore these plays from the audience's perspective. Then we shift to the viewpoint of the performer, describing how performers train and prepare to stage a play.

Chapter 1 delves into the rich history of nō, tracing its evolution from its ritualistic origins to its contemporary practice. We begin by exploring the art's roots in ancient ceremonies and the influence of earlier performing arts. We then focus on the transformative innovations of actors and playwrights Kan'ami (1333–1384) and Zeami (1363 or 1364–1443?), who established the basic elements of nō dramaturgy and stage conventions. We then examine the development of nō, including its relationship to political institutions, such as patronage by the ruling class, and its popularization among various social classes, which may have led to adaptations for the commoners. Finally, we will look at how nō has changed since the opening of Japan to the West and subsequent modernization, tracing its path to its current form.

Chapter 2 offers a comprehensive overview of the nō repertory. We explore different methods of play categorization and analyze common dramaturgical structures and plot types, providing numerous examples. Our discussion delves into key dramaturgical features and recurring themes, such as the dynamic between the *shite* and *waki* characters, the use of travel motifs, and patterns of "disguise and revelation." Additionally, we examine storytelling techniques and the literary characteristics of nō, including the diverse sources from which plays are derived.

Chapter 3 explores the interplay between visual aspects of nō performance and their connection to the play's themes. We analyze the unique nō stage, followed by a look at how movement—posture, gait, and stylized patterns (*kata*)—creates the distinctive nō dance. We explore the visual symbolism of masks, costumes, and fans, and how they are used to enhance the narrative. Then, we examine how stage properties contribute to storytelling within the performance.

Finally, a short conclusion presents current issues in the world of nō, and sketches trajectories for future developments.

Formerly known as *sarugaku*, nō emerged in the early fourteenth century thanks in part to the artistry of actor-playwrights such as Kan'ami and his son Zeami and has been continuously transmitted to the present day by communities of professional and amateur practitioners from various social classes, from the cultural and political elite to the commoners. The core elements that define nō dramaturgy and performance were established in the Muromachi period (1336–1573), a time of great aesthetic development despite political instability, during which other traditional arts, such as the tea ceremony, also emerged. However, throughout its long history nō has evolved in response to different socioeconomic and cultural contexts, constantly updating its performance techniques and, to some extent, its repertory.

About 240 plays are currently performed, with the majority of them having been written during the Muromachi period. About half of them are particularly popular with contemporary audiences and are therefore performed more often. The nō repertory is diverse, drawing on classical literature, religious scriptures, and oral myths and legends. Its characters include aristocrats, warriors, and court ladies, as well as deities, demons, ghosts, plant spirits, and mythical animals. This reflects nō's heterogeneous influences, including agricultural rituals, demon-quelling ceremonies, musical storytelling, didactic pantomime, narrative dance, and more.

Performances last between one and two hours on average and are characterized by the use of lavish costumes and sophisticated masks that stand out against the simple backdrop of the nō stage, a bare wooden structure with no scenery (see Figure 1). Actors and musicians dedicate their careers to mastering and performing the repertory. Similarly, nō enthusiasts often attend several performances a month, developing a deep familiarity with the recurring characters, stories, and staging elements. This leads to a shared knowledge of nō culture within a community that includes professionals, amateurs, and audiences who influence each other and enhance the overall appreciation of the art form.

Nō is performed in conjunction with kyōgen (lit. "crazy words"), its comedic counterpart, and together they are known as nōgaku, a term that started to be used in the Meiji

FIGURE 1 *Outdoor performance of* Hagoromo. Shite: *Kongō Tatsunori. Fushimi Inari Taisha, Kyoto. September 8, 2017. Photograph: Fabio Massimo Fioravanti.*

period (1868–1912). Since two to three nō plays, in addition to kyōgen, are usually performed on the same day, audiences have the opportunity to experience the diverse repertory. It is quite possible, for example, to see a play featuring the stately dance of a deity, then move on to a more "realistic" play set in the world of the samurai, and conclude with a spectacular play with mythical beasts and acrobatic movements. Not all nō plays are equally accessible, however. While some are relatively fast-paced, with numerous exchanges between characters and action sequences, others are more static, focusing more on individual narration or abstract dance. Some plays may tell stories that are deeply rooted in local culture or removed from the everyday experiences of the audience, while others may deal with "universal" human themes that are shared across time and space. Similarly, the many literary, religious, and historical references that are woven into nō plays may require some background knowledge to be identified and fully appreciated. Other plays, however, can be enjoyed without needing to access all the nuances of the text because of the prominence of visual or choreographic elements.

Narratives in nō plays often appear deceptively simple, featuring a main character, the *shite* (pronounced sh'tay, lit. "doer"), and a secondary character, the *waki* (lit. "side"). These may have supporting characters (*tsure and waki tsure*) whose dramatic roles are usually limited.[1] The essential dramatic tension arises from the interaction between the *shite* and the *waki*. Within this structure, the *shite* is the narrative center from which all action develops. One does not watch nō to enjoy the intricacies of the story, as one would in other traditional Japanese theatre forms such as kabuki and bunraku, which feature large numbers of characters and multiple layers of plot and subplot. Rather, the beauty of nō plays lies in the simplicity of their stories, which revolve around a single narrative core. Most nō plays are named after the *shite* (e.g., *Atsumori*, *Kiyotsune*, *Tōru*), after a specific place associated with such characters (e.g., *Takasago*, *Nonomiya*, *Sumidagawa*), or after a key object associated with such characters (e.g., *Izutsu* [*The Well Curb*], *Funa Benkei* [*Benkei on the Boat*], *Sesshōseki* [*The Killing Stone*]). The thematic coherence of nō plays, achieved through the interweaving of intertextual references all pointing to a single semantic core, is what Ezra Pound (1885–1972), in his pioneering exploration of nō, called "the unity of image."[2] Indeed, the minimalism of its plots as well as its performance conventions are among the features of nō that attracted the interest of Western modernist theatre practitioners and played a role in introducing nō to international audiences.

A particularly relevant feature of nō is the peculiar dramatic structure found in numerous nō plays, known as *mugen* ("dream and illusion"). In such plays, the main character is a ghost or spirit who appears to the *waki* in disguise in the first act (*mae shite*) and then reveals their true self in the second act (*nochi shite*) to recount a significant past event in their lives, which is often the source of emotional distress. This act of storytelling allows the *shite* to free themselves from attachments that hinder their path to Buddhist salvation. In *mugen* plays, the focus is on narrating and re-enacting the past, with the *waki* as the initiator and witness of the storytelling. Such plays function as requiems or memorials for the *shite*, following the concept of *chinkon*: rituals intended to pacify troubled spirits. *Atsumori*, one of the pieces we analyze in this book, is a prime example of this type of nō.

Although deeply rooted in the cultural context in which it was created and developed, the stylized, abstract expressiveness of both its texts and its staging allows different audiences to engage with the stories it presents. Like all masterpieces of theatre, nō plays have the power to memorialize specific events, but they also serve as parables that show us the cyclical recurrence of human experience.[3]

The narrative coherence of nō plays arises not only from the minimalism of the plots but also from the interweaving of related images in a process akin to syntactic coordination rather than subordination. The "tapestry of nō" is a metaphorical expression referred to as the elaborate interweaving of literary, choreographic, visual, and aural elements into a unified performance text in which word cannot be separated from gesture, and sound cannot be separated from sight.

The great authors who composed what later became the canon of nō plays had specific stage conventions in mind, including dance, music, and movement. Zeami, the actor/playwright credited for having innovated the art of nō in the early Muromachi period left numerous writings on his art. In *Fūshi kaden* (*Transmitting the Flower Through Effects and Attitudes*) he warns against writing one-dimensional plays:

> What we need are plays in which the movement is matched to the singing of the text. This is a matter of great difficulty. These are the plays that really excite an audience's interest. The language should be easily understood, and individual words should hold interest; the melody should be attractive, and the flow from word to word, graceful; special care

> should be taken to include points of concentrated interest that can be enacted with strong visual appeal. This is how to write. When all these elements are suitable to one another, the entire audience is excited.[4]

It is clear that, since Zeami's time, nō has been a deeply intermedial art, meaning that multiple levels of the performance text are expressed through different media (including words, music, choreography, stage properties, masks, and costumes) that are deeply interdependent and constantly interacting with each other.[5] For instance, the lines of the characters are composed to be sung to a specific kind of music, which in turn is paired with the movements of the actor. In this complex relationship, there is no defined hierarchy of performance elements. Sometimes the music leads, sometimes the movement, sometimes everything stops to make room for *utai* (sung poetry). The Western avant-garde practitioners of the early twentieth century (William Butler Yeats, Paul Claudel, Bertolt Brecht, etc.) sought inspiration in nō theatre's "holistic" approach to dramaturgy as an alternative to Western theatrical conventions based on the primacy of the text.

All aspects of nō composition and performance are meticulously regulated. To understand this, it is essential to introduce the Japanese concept of *kata*, a word which can be translated as "model," "form," or "pattern," but also as "direction" or "method." In the context of nō, the word *kata* can refer to any established element that contributes to the production of a piece. How to walk on stage, how to sing a line, how to carve a mask, these are all *kata*: that is, they do not depend on the improvisation or creativity of an individual but are prescribed by tradition and shared by a community of practice. *Kata* are embodied by the performers who have mastered them. These forms and methods are passed down within kinship groups that form stylistic schools (*ryūgi*), each of which carries the knowledge of a specific nō practice and is sanctioned by the *iemoto*, the highest authority in each school. *Kata* constitute the ethos of a school and form a kind of "common performative language" that needs to be shared by all members of the community: It is therefore imperative that they be respected and protected. However, the content of these forms is not immutable. While the texts of the plays have remained largely unchanged since their composition, their performance conventions have evolved thanks to the creativity of individuals who gradually modified these forms to suit the tastes of the audience. Being aware of the tension between the need to preserve and the need to innovate is key to understanding how nō has been transmitted and how it will develop in the future.

From play structure to music, from choreography to the use of masks and costumes, virtually every aspect of nō is based to some degree on the repetition of a form. As we explain in Chapter 1, nō underwent stages of canonization of its repertory and techniques. However, it was this standardization that facilitated the emergence of numerous variations and exceptions, thus expanding nō's expressive capabilities.

A clear example of this adaptability in nō is the existence of *kogaki*, or staging variations, for almost every play. Developed primarily during the Edo period (1603–1868), these variants can significantly alter elements such as the choice of mask and costume, as well as the structure, text, and movement of a play. Notably, special permission is required to perform *kogaki*, reflecting their perceived complexity and advanced nature compared to standard versions. This speaks to the inherent hierarchy of elements within nō, known as *kurai*, a term indicating the "gravitas" or "weight" of performance. Plays with a lower *kurai*, such as *Atsumori*, are easier to stage and can be performed by younger actors, while plays with a higher *kurai*, such as *Sumidagawa*, require more experience.

Prescribed variations and stylistic differences between schools and performers are ways of making old things new. In the highly canonized context of nō, uniformity to a single aesthetic standard would likely lead to extinction. On the contrary, nō tries to create a fresh experience in each production, following the *ichi-go ichi-e* ("one time, one meeting") principle, which refers to the fact that each act of people meeting other people is unique and unrepeatable. Unlike other forms of theatre, where a performance is collectively rehearsed and then staged over a period ranging from a few days to many years, nō performances are one-time events. It seems that nō has developed a structured approach that emphasizes the essential characteristics of any performance: its ephemerality and irreproducibility.[6]

Watching nō

In this section we provide an account of the experience of watching a performance of the famous plays *Atsumori*, set during the twelfth-century conflict between two rival clans, the Taira and the Minamoto (see Figures 6 and 7 in Chapter 3), and *Sumidagawa*, telling the story of a mother on a journey to find her missing child (see Figures 8 and 9 in Chapter 3).

Most nō plays are performed in special halls known as *nōgakudō*. Upon entering the performance space, the audience's eyes are drawn to the nō stage, an elegant structure made of natural wood (*hinoki*) and covered by a roof. The central performance area is a square stage, with a bridgeway (*hashigakari*) extending from stage right. At the back is a painting of a pine tree, which remains the same regardless of which play is being performed. At the far end hangs a five-colored curtain (*age maku*). Figure 2 is a top view of the stage showing its different areas.

The audience surrounds the stage, with seating divided into three areas: the front, the left side in front of the *hashigakari* but facing it, and a wedge-shaped area in between. The audience should be careful in their choice of where to sit: The pillar supporting the roof below stage right may partially obstruct the view. Despite modern adaptations, such as moving the stage indoors and illuminating it with artificial lighting, there remain parts of the performance that will not be visible, or

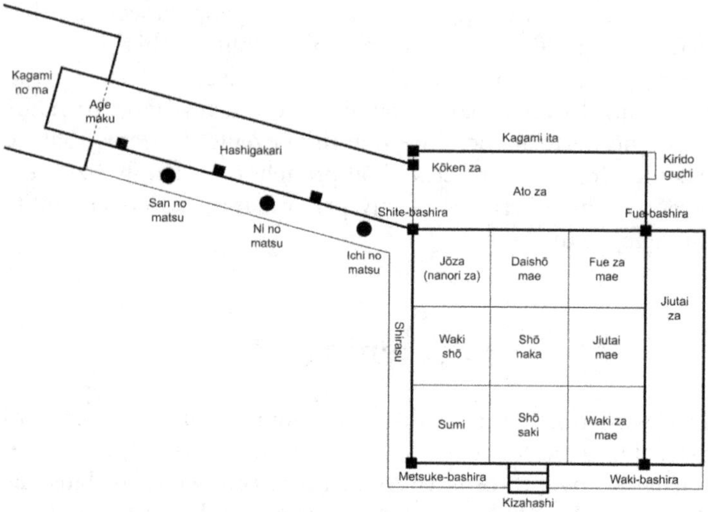

FIGURE 2 *Diagram of a nō stage with names of areas and other structural elements.*

parts of the lines that may not be fully audible to the audience. Nō seems to invite us to embrace this inherent incompleteness in our perception.

Nō theatre halls are medium-sized venues (about 500 seats), and the audience is largely made up of frequent theatregoers, many of them amateur practitioners who may have come to watch their teacher on stage. Amidst the lingering buzz, the solemn tones of a flute is heard from behind the curtain (*age maku*). Soon the rhythmic beats of the drums follow. This opening music (*oshirabe*) serves not only as a brief warm-up for the instrumentalists, but also to draw the attention and focus of the actors and audience to the performance. The stage is bare, but the audience can already sense the mood of the play.

Soon after the music stops, instrumentalists dressed in black kimono bearing their family crests emerge from behind the curtain and walk in a line toward the main stage. As they enter, the audience is still. The only sounds are the soft shuffling of *tabi* (white split-toed socks) on wood and the rustling of silk *hakama* (divided skirt). The instrumentalists reach their positions at the back of the stage (*ato za*) and sit down. From the *kirido-guchi*, eight chorus singers emerge and sit with folded legs (*seiza*) in two rows facing the center of the stage at *jiutai za*. As the drummers unfold and sit on their stools, the chorus members meticulously arrange their fans. A deep silence, charged with anticipation, has enveloped the room. Finally, this silence is broken by the sound of the flute and the raw sounds of the drums, the percussionists punctuating the beat with sharp, high-pitched vocalizations. This is the beginning of the first act (*maeba*).

Suddenly, the curtain is lifted, revealing a figure in a muted kimono and a distinctive long-finned hood. He is not wearing a mask, but his face is expressionless. He walks to the stage as the music accompanies him. He is the *waki*, the supporting actor who often appears first on stage. His costume reveals his identity as a monk: He holds a fan in his right hand and prayer beads in his left. His feet, covered in white *tabi*, glide by in a perfectly controlled motion, almost like a statue being carried along on a conveyor belt. The monk faces the musicians and sings a short chant in a low, quiet tone. When the song ends, he turns to the audience and explains his identity and situation.

The monk is now known as Renshō, but he once was called Kumagai Naozane, a warrior of the Minamoto clan. He speaks of his remorse for killing Taira no Atsumori, a young member of the enemy clan, the Taira, at the Ichinotani in Suma (present-day Kobe). Renshō is now traveling to Suma to hold a memorial service for Atsumori. On stage, without physically moving, he sings a travel song (*michiyuki*), in which it is customary to mention landmarks encountered along the way. Overwhelmed by the serene landscape of Suma, so different from the war scenes of his past, he mentions hearing flute sounds.

Soon the shrill sound of the flute pierces the air. This is the formal opening of this kind of entrance music that is also common to other plays, but one can imagine a semantic connection to the theme of the flute. The drums begin to play a slow, hypnotic pattern in a loop. Then the curtain lifts gently to reveal four actors dressed in green and blue kimono-like costumes, each carrying a stick with grass tied to the end (see Figure 6 in Chapter 3). Since nō does not use background set design, the costumes seem to transform the otherwise bare wooden stage into a canvas painted with green and blue, colors that evoke the natural landscape of Suma Bay.

The four characters are the *mae shite* (main character in the first act) and three *tsure* (supporting actors) representing the grass cutters of Suma Bay. They sing in unison, describing the melancholy of this neglected province. For those with background knowledge, the word "Suma" immediately conjures up images of a lonely existence far from the bustling capital. These associations are deeply rooted in traditional arts and are deliberately woven into the fabric of the play. Lines are often delivered in verse and make ample use of poetic language, frequently quoting directly from classical literature, which can make their meaning difficult to understand, particularly when delivered as chant. Some in the audience may follow the play while reading from a chant book (*utaibon*), while others may be less concerned with parsing each syllable and more focused on participating in the performance.

The monk praises the grass cutters for their refined flute playing, though such an art seems unusual for their humble status, but the *shite* counters that the poems celebrate the grass cutters' flute and the woodcutter's songs, challenging the notion that elegance is reserved for the highborn. In fact, what is shown on stage seems to visualize only the traditional perspective of the noble observing the humble: that is, depicting the elegant pastoral scenes found in court poetry without offering a realistic depiction of poverty. The chorus (*jiutai*) sings in response to the *shite*'s words, mentioning the names of famous flutes. At the same time, the *shite* moves around the stage in a circular pattern, his gestures accentuated by his right hand holding a bamboo stick into which grass has been inserted. Finally, he asks the monk to pray for him, subtly revealing his identity as the ghost of Atsumori before disappearing.

Meanwhile, three stage assistants (*kōken*) have been sitting at the back of the stage, facing forward. Although they may appear passive, their roles are crucial to the performance. The *kōken* are other *shite* actors from the same group, responsible for a variety of onstage and backstage tasks, including dressing the actors, preparing props, making costume adjustments, or discreetly passing items to performers. In addition, the *kōken* play a vital role in maintaining the continuity of the performance. They are prepared to step in in the event of an accident, including taking over the role of *shite*, should he or she be unable to continue. Like the ritual summoning of a spirit, a nō performance, once initiated, should be brought to completion.

As the grass cutter (*shite*) retreats backstage, the first act ends. Some in the audience will follow his figure as he quietly walks along the bridgeway, while others may be comfortably asleep. There are certain aspects of nō performance that elicit this kind of response: In addition to the comfortable chairs and air conditioning, there is the repetitiveness or predictability of the action, and also the hypnotic looping of the drums. Each element is meticulously predetermined, yet each performer brings a unique and individual interpretation to the script. While newcomers might initially perceive the uniformity and repetition as uninteresting, a deeper understanding and experience reveal the intricate subtleties and variations that distinguish each piece and performance.

When the grass cutter returns to the backstage, a local man appears. At the request of the monk, he tells the story of Atsumori's death at the hands of Naozane. This is the *ai kyōgen* interlude, drawn from the military chronicle *The Tale of the Heike*. This epic tale describes the war between the Minamoto (also known as Genji) and Taira (also known as Heike) clans for control of Japan, culminating in the Taira's downfall. The story is uniquely told from the perspective of the defeated Taira, romanticizing their defeat, and serving as a grim reminder that even those who once flourished are doomed to disappear. The local man relates how, as the Minamoto clan swarmed through the Taira camp at Ichinotani, Naozane confronted Atsumori. Realizing that his opponent was only sixteen, Naozane hesitated, but finally decided to take Atsumori's life in a dignified manner before other warriors reached them. This tragic episode led him to renounce the world and embrace Buddhism, taking the name Renshō.

Following the advice of the local man, the monk begins to pray for the spirit of Atsumori. The second act (*nochi ba*) has begun. As the instrumentalists play, the curtain slowly rises to reveal a beautifully dressed warrior (see Figure 7 in Chapter 3). He wears a mask that represents the elegant features of a young Taira clansman. This is the *shite* of the second act (*nochi shite*), the ghost of Atsumori, performed by the same actor who appeared in the first act. He slowly crosses the bridge and confronts the monk, thanking him for his prayers. He explains that the two of them, who were enemies in the past, have become companions in Buddhism. Atsumori sits on a black lacquered barrel and sings about the Buddhist concept of the impermanence of all things, exchanging lines with the chorus. Then he stands and begins to gesture with his fan while the chorus sings its lines. In this central section of the play, called *kuse*, Atsumori tells how his clan the Taira, once prosperous, was defeated by the rival Minamoto and forced to live as humble fishermen in Suma Bay.

Watching Atsumori reflect on his last night at the camp, where his men sought solace in music and recalled their glory days at the capital, brings back memories for Renshō as well. As he camped nearby, he remembers the haunting sound of a flute he could hear coming from the enemy's quarters. Atsumori then performs the *chū no mai*, a dance with instrumental music. Although not explicitly stated in the script, it is possible to see this as an interpretation of how Atsumori played the flute and danced that night, suggesting that this dance could be a reenactment of those moments. The repetitive flute and percussion patterns induce a trance-like state in the audience, further immersing them in the imaginative experience.

After the dance, the chant picks up speed, with Atsumori's movements shifting from abstract to more mimetic, illustrating how his clan retreated by boat. He was about to flee to the sea on horseback when Naozane confronted him. The ensuing fight scene includes Naozane's gesture of spreading his fan and calling out to his enemy, Atsumori turning with his horse's reins in his hand, their exchange of blows, and their wrestling that leads to Atsumori being thrown from his horse to the ground. All of this is performed by the *shite* accompanied by narration by the chorus. Atsumori then raises his fan to reveal the image of the sun setting in the waves, symbolizing his demise. Reflecting on his past, the ghost is about to strike the monk with his sword, but he stops when he realizes Renshō's long-standing remorse over Atsumori's death. Recognizing that their enmity has dissolved and that they are destined for the Pure Land Paradise, the scene ends on a note of reconciliation.

The audience remain silent as the *shite* closes his fan and quietly leaves the stage to return to the world behind the curtain. The musicians fold up their stools and the chorus is ready to leave, just as they came, but this time there is a general sense of uplift, brought on by the resolution of the story. As the silence lingers, some begin to applaud. In nō, it is customary for there to be only brief applause as the cast retreats backstage, never to return to the stage for a "curtain call." This highlights the ritual dimension of nō, emphasizing the performers' role as vehicles through which characters are summoned, and stories are re-presented on stage.

In a typical day of nō, it is customary to stage a full kyōgen play and/or some *shimai* (excerpts from a full play) between two nō. This provides some relief from the relative "weight" of the nō plays, while also allowing other performers to participate in the event. During this time, some members of the audience will take a break, leaving the hall or chatting in the lobby before the next performance begins.

Atsumori is a typical example of *mugen* nō, but not all plays follow this structure. *Sumidagawa*, written by Zeami's son Motomasa (1394?–1432), is one of several *genzai* ("present time") nō plays that depict a character in a deranged mental state resulting from some form of emotional trauma, such as the loss of a family member. In these plays the *shite* often goes on a journey to find the lost one, usually ending with a joyful reunion, except for *Sumidagawa*.

This play begins with the introduction of a ferryman (*waki*) who carries people across the Sumida River in present-day Tokyo. A traveler (*waki tsure*) returning from the capital (Kyoto) arrives, followed by a woman in a state of mental distress (*shite*, see Figure 8 in Chapter 3). She wears a round lacquered hat and a simple, plain-colored robe, signifying that she is traveling. She also carries a bamboo branch, a convention indicating her deranged mental state. Her son was kidnapped by slave traders who took him to the eastern provinces, and she cannot be at peace until she finds him. She asks to board the boat, but the ferryman insists that she must entertain him first. The woman sings, quoting "Miyako Birds" (Birds of the Capital), a famous poem, and convinces the ferryman to let her on board. This is a common trope in madness plays, as in medieval Japan there was little distinction between the ravings of a madman and the antics of entertainers.

As they approach the shore, the woman notices a crowd around a willow tree on the other side of the river and inquiries about them. The ferryman explains that they are holding a Buddhist memorial service (*dainenbutsu*) to pray for the soul of a child who was kidnapped by slave traders, then died, and is now buried under the tree. When she questions the ferrymen further, the woman realizes that the child is her son, Umewakamaru, and breaks down in tears (see Figure 9 left in Chapter 3). As darkness falls, the memorial service begins. The boat reaches the opposite shore, and the woman joins in. Suddenly, a voice echoes from the mound, and the ghost of Umewakamaru (who sometimes appears on stage as *kokata* [child actor]) materializes (see Figure 9 right in Chapter 3). Overwhelmed with disbelief and joy at seeing her son, the woman tries to embrace him, but he slips through her and disappears into his grave. By dawn, only wild grasses remain on the mound.

The atmosphere, heavily charged with the aftermath of the performance, lingers so powerfully that the audience struggles to get up from their seats. The chorus sings a short song, an excerpt from a first-category piece, so as not to destroy the atmosphere, but at the same time to relieve the pressure that came with the dramatic story of *Sumidagawa*. The audience leaves the hall, and the stage has returned to its original state of emptiness, ready for another cycle to begin.

Now that we have a better idea of how performances appear from the audience's point of view, we will try to switch sides and take a look at how actors and musicians prepare for the staging of a play.

Practicing nō

The day of a nō performance begins in the backstage area (*gakuya*), a series of interconnected empty rooms with *tatami* (straw mat) floors. The rooms are populated by actors and musicians, all dressed in formal black silk kimono and *hakama*. Like the stage, the backstage area is completely empty before and after the performance. Properties, if used, are prepared for the performance, then dismantled and stored until the next production. Costumes and masks, which are extremely valuable items, are usually brought in by the actors, who may own them or may rent them for the occasion. If the actor also owns or manages the theatre, these items may be stored in a vault connected to the stage area. Similarly, drummers bring the various parts of their instruments, which they assemble and tune just before the performance begins. In sum, preparations for a performance are made by the performers themselves; there are no stagehands or resident technical staff working at a nō theatre.

Both young and experienced actors share not only the stage proper but also the backstage area. Here, the actors taking the roles of *shite* and *tsure* prepare by donning their costumes under the guidance of three fellow *shite* actors taking the role of assistants (*kōken*). They begin the dressing process with a padded white silk undergarment designed to increase the volume of the upper body, a fundamental aspect of their transformation. The dressing process is meticulous: Layers of silk are carefully aligned and secured with knots and stitches. Although the costumes are made to predetermined sizes, they are expertly adjusted to fit each performer's body. When not worn, these costumes appear flat and shapeless. Part of a *shite* actor's training includes mastering the care of these garments and the complex techniques required to give them three-dimensionality and character-specific shape.

The preparation of the masks is equally precise. The actors place small fabric or paper pads (*men ate*) in the back of the mask, not only for comfort but also to create a necessary gap between the face and the mask, which aids breathing and enhances vocal resonance. *Men ate* also influence the angle of the mask, which is critical because both lighting and viewing perspective significantly influence how the mask is perceived.

Once dressed, the *shite* is led by the *kōken* to the *kagami no ma*, the mirror room just behind the five-colored curtain. Here, seated on a stool and facing a mirror, the *shite* awaits the arrival of the musicians and other performers, responding to their greetings only with a nod, otherwise maintaining a solemn silence. It is before this mirror that the final element of the transformation takes place: the donning of the mask. The *shite* reverently greets the mask with a bow and then, with the help of the *kōken*, secures it with braided silk cords. This moment marks the completion of the transformation. It should be noted that neither costumes nor masks are used in practice or rehearsal, offering the actor the only glimpse of their full character embodiment before a performance. Meanwhile, the *waki* has entered the stage and introduced the story. As the musicians begin to play the *shite*'s entrance music, the backstage lights are turned off. At the established musical cue, the *shite* calls for the curtain to be raised. The stage lights illuminate the *kagami no ma*, and the journey of the *shite* begins.

One of the surprising facts about nō production is that the cast of a nō performance does not rehearse together but meets only for a single "dry run" (*mōshiawase*) a few days before the event. How is it possible that such a complex art, in which every movement is carefully choreographed and every note is synchronized, can be performed without a long period of collective rehearsal? Let us take a step back and understand who a nō performer is, how they train, and how they prepare for a performance.

Professional performers, or *nōgakushi*, are divided into four main categories: *shite kata*, who perform the roles of *shite*, *tsure*, *kōken*, and also sing in the chorus; *waki kata*, who perform the roles of *waki* and *waki tsure*; *hayashi kata* (musicians), further divided into flute, shoulder drum, hip drum, and stick drum players; and *kyōgen kata*, who are comic actors.[7] Each performer specializes exclusively in a single role and does not engage in any professional practices other than nō. Traditionally, nō has been predominantly male, although there has recently been a notable increase in the number of female performers, reflecting both historical and sociological changes. Performers are organized into stylistic schools or *ryūgi*, such as five schools of *shite*, three of *waki*, fourteen of instruments (in all), etc., each maintaining a distinct style but sharing much of the same repertory, emphasizing the stylistic fragmentation characteristic of nō. These schools are family-based, with traditions passed down through generations. Each is led by a Grandmaster (*iemoto*), who represents the apex of artistic and political authority within the school and ensures the continuity of the legacy. Although there is communication and collaboration among the schools, specialists from the same role but different schools do not perform together, thus preserving the unique identity of each.

The status of a professional performer within the nō community is not only recognized by peers but is also formally acknowledged through membership in the Nohgaku Professionals' Association (Nōgaku Kyōkai). This endorsement serves both as a mark of social recognition and also has economic reasons. Given the nature of the nō production and performance system, only a few professionals can rely solely on performing as their primary source of income. As a result, most of them base their livelihoods on teaching amateurs. Unlike many modern performing arts, nō maintains a traditional structure in which performers work as freelancers within family-based groups. They collaborate to manage all aspects of production, from costumes and masks to theatre buildings and performance schedules. This system emphasizes mutual support over competition, with roles assigned by seniority and rank rather than audition.

The training system for *shite* actors, who make up the majority of the nō population, begins early, often around the age of 3 for those born into professional families. These young trainees participate in child actor roles (*kokata*) alongside veteran actors, and gradually progress to performing on stage with adults as they master parts of the repertory. This path is also open to those outside the tradition through study with professional actors, with many beginning their journey in university nō clubs and later choosing to pursue nō as a profession. The training emphasizes specialization, but includes a basic understanding of all nō arts, which is essential for performing in a field that operates without directors or conductors, and without a collective rehearsal process.

The curriculum varies by specialization and stylistic school, though it is based on similar principles, with trainees typically under the guidance of a single mentor, possibly studying directly under the *iemoto*. The relationship with this mentor is exclusive and determines the trainee's involvement in performance until independence, signified by mastery of several key pieces, such as *Shakkyō*, *Midare* (a variant of *Shōjō*), and *Dōjōji*.

Training methods focus on one-on-one instruction in repertory, from simple song and dance excerpts to complex pieces and complete plays. Nō training (*keiko*) does not involve physical exercises or movement routines but is always based on the study and memorization of a play or parts of a play for the purpose of performance. It is a form of "situated learning" in which participation in the performance is an integral part of the training, with roles ranging from backstage and onstage assistants (*kōken*) to chorus members and supporting characters.[8]

Performers practice the nō canon throughout their lives. Therefore, preparation for a particular piece does not start when the performance schedule is set, but is based on accumulated knowledge and experience, beginning in childhood, and including participation in various production roles through adult performances. Training involves the study of dance excerpts (*shimai*), participating as a chorus member, serving as a stage assistant, and playing the role of *tsure*. This extensive background allows the actor's memorization of numerous chants and movement, which are practiced individually until the collective fine-tuning in the dry run.

It is also likely that the *shite* has taught the play several times to amateur students or junior actors. For plays that are being studied for the first time, the actors memorize the script using chant books, with the music possibly annotated separately. Once the script is completely memorized, including the lines of the *waki* and the chorus, movement training (*tachi-geiko*) begins, using *kata tsuke*, documents that annotate movement sequences, either hand-copied from the teacher or *iemoto*, or learned from videos of past performances. This phase of training is usually solitary and culminates in a presentation to a teacher, senior member, or the *iemoto* for feedback.

The final step before the public performance is the dry run (*mōshiawase*), which is done without costumes or masks and does not include the entire performance; this session is crucial to ensuring that the independently prepared parts harmonize effectively, although the *mōshiawase* is sometimes skipped. This approach to production reflects the nō principle of being over-trained yet under-rehearsed. As already mentioned, the goal is to maximize the freshness of performance, even when the piece is classical and the performance methods are traditional and familiar to everyone. The tension between form and application of form, which leaves room for interpretation but also for human error, is key to understanding the beauty of nō.

1

History

Origins

Perfected over 650 years ago by the playwrights Kan'ami (also known as Kanze Kiyotsugu, 1333–1384) and his son Zeami (also known as Kanze Motokiyo, or Hada Motokiyo, 1363 or 1364-1443?), nō has been handed down continuously to the present day. Research, however, suggests that the art form as we know it today has undergone gradual changes throughout its long history. Performing arts inherently reflect the zeitgeist of their era, and in this sense nō has remained a "contemporary" form of performance for over six centuries: Its aesthetics, as well as the socioeconomic relationships between performers and patrons, have changed in response to shifting historical contexts. This chapter looks at how nō has evolved across cultures and time periods, examining its social, political, religious, and artistic influences. We explore how nō reflected and shaped the values, beliefs, and identities of its audiences, and how it interacted with other forms of art, media, and entertainment. We also discuss the challenges and innovations in nō production and performance, providing a comprehensive overview of how nō developed through the ages.

Ritual origins

Until the Meiji era (1868–1912), the art of nō was known as *sarugaku* or *sarugaku no nō* (lit. "the nō of *sarugaku*"). The character for *saru* means "monkey," while *gaku* means both "music" and "dance." The origin of this expression and its meaning are unclear, but it might lead to the assumption that *sarugaku* involved some form of *imitation*, similar to the behavior of a *monkey*. The character for *nō* means "ability" or "talent." Although there is no definitive theory as to how it was used in this context, the word "nō" may have indicated dramatic performances, featuring characters and some degree of plot, staged by groups of entertainers, among which were *sarugaku* performers. The word "nō" started to appear in the Kamakura period (1185–1333), but historical research suggests that the origins of nō go back about 1,300 years, when *sarugaku* evolved from *sangaku*, a mixed art that included circus acrobatics as well as short comical skits, that was introduced from mainland China and the Korean peninsula and was staged as part of Buddhist ceremonies.

In the fourth century, Japan formed an alliance with the Korean kingdom of Paekche (18 BC–AD 660) to counter the threat of Silla, a coalition of kingdoms on the Korean peninsula. Around 552 or 538, during the Asuka period (538–710), Buddhism was officially introduced to Japan. This occurred when King Seong of Baekje (504–554) presented the twenty-ninth Japanese Emperor Kinmei (509–571) with a Buddha statue, scriptures, and other valuable items to symbolize their alliance. Despite initial opposition from powerful clans who followed the cult of *kami* (native Japanese deities), Buddhism gradually gained official recognition. This was especially evident during the reign of Japan's first female ruler, Empress Suiko (593–628) and her nephew Prince Shōtoku (also known as Umayado, 574–622), who served as regent.

According to the Taihō Code of 701,[1] among the eight national ministries established according to the Chinese administrative model was the *gagaku ryō* (Bureau of Court Music), an institution responsible for overseeing court music and dance that operated under the Civil Administration Office (*jibusho*). Foreign performers were invited as instructors to train Japanese artists in various continental music and dance forms from China and Korea, as well as *sangaku*. These forms of music and dance eventually became known as *gagaku* and *bugaku*, respectively. It was widely believed that Chinese music and dance known as *gigaku* were precursors of nō. However, the *gigaku* performance tradition quickly disappeared, and today only a few of its masks survive. Based on limited textual evidence, it is theorized that the *gigaku* may have included pantomimes from various Asian regions, such as Turkey, Mongolia, Tibet, and India. These performances were probably introduced to Japan through international exchanges along the Silk Road.

In China and Korea, *sangaku* was known as *bay xi* (lit. "one hundred entertainments"), a generic term for folk performing arts as opposed to those of the court. As far as can be determined from the paintings on bows preserved in the Shōsōin repository in Nara, *sangaku* in Japan were circus-like shows, including magic tricks and acrobatics. There was also an official register of *sangaku* performers (*sangakko*) administered by the government in Nara as part of the *gagaku ryō*. *Sangaku*, which had been patronized by the state as a performing art, was performed at Buddhist ceremonies. Although the *sangakko* was dismantled in 782, *sangaku* spread throughout Japan as an entertainment for the masses. The reason for its loss of aristocratic patronage was due to its miscellaneous nature and sometimes unrefined style.

In the Heian period (794–1185), the term *sarugaku* or *sarugō-gamashii* (acting like *sarugaku*) was commonly used among the aristocracy to refer to humorous acting or behavior. However, it was not only the nobility who appreciated the comic theatre of *sarugaku*. The fictional diary *Shin Sarugakuki* (*An Account of New Sarugaku*), written by the scholar Fujiwara Akihira (989–1066), depicts scenes of watching *sarugaku* performances in the streets, presumably attended by people from all walks of life. These performers may have been the remnants of the dispersed *sangaku* troupes that had lost the patronage of the state. The titles of these plays, such as "A Virtuous Nun Begging for Diapers," "Pranks of Kyoto Youth," and "An Eastern Country Bumpkin's First Visit to the Capital," give us an idea of their subject matter. These comical skits, which involved mimicking various characters, were well-suited to being called "*sarugaku*" (meaning "monkey music and dance"). The diary records that the audience found these plays extremely amusing, further supporting the idea that Heian-era *sarugaku* was a form of comedy. It has been argued that these sketches may have been the forerunners of modern kyōgen, which, if true, would position kyōgen as an early ancestor of nō.

Comic *sarugaku* continued to be performed during the Kamakura period (1185–1333). In his diary the courtier Asukai Masa'ari (1241–1301, also known as Gayū) notes that the losing team in *kemari* (an ancient soccer game played at the imperial court) was required to perform *sarugaku* as a form of penalty during banquets.[2] At the same time, from the late Heian period onward, *sarugaku* underwent a significant transformation. There are records of it being staged in temples and shrines. However, characterizing *sarugaku* as a religious play is complicated by the diversity of its forms and performers. Another stage art known as *ennen* (literally, "longevity") encompassed a variety of performing arts, including *sarugaku*, and was often staged by priests as entertainment following Buddhist services. *Ennen* may have included performances such as *furyū* and *renji*, which involved dramatic forms with chanted dialogue. Some scholars have suggested that these may be related to the development of *sarugaku no nō* as a dialogue-based form of poetic drama.

Other notable examples of how *sarugaku* performances were used are the rituals known as *shushōe* and *shunie*. Still performed in temples and shrines on New Year's Day and at various points in February in the lunar calendar, these ceremonies aim to banish the misfortunes of the previous year and pray for a good harvest. At the end of the ceremony, a form of dramatized prayer is performed to drive away *oni* (demons or evil spirits) through the power of Buddhist deities. Religious institutions hired *sarugaku* performers to portray the demons more realistically. Famous for their mimetic skills, *sarugaku* performers excelled at depicting a range of characters, including gods and demons, often with more finesse than the monks. This led to the integration of *sarugaku* into Buddhist ceremonies, with performers using masks to bring these supernatural roles to life. It was the beginning of the development of *sarugaku* into a form of masked drama.

In addition to the primary roles in the *shushōe* and *shunie* ceremonies, *sarugaku* actors also performed special roles known as *shushi*. These originated from the practices of yin-yang divination that governed the magical aspects of the ritual, and included running around the prayer hall, an act believed to dispel evil spirits and purify the area. It is thought that the involvement of *sarugaku* performers in these actions helped to enhance the mystical aura of the rituals.[3] This illustrates the evolution of *sarugaku* from comic sketches to solemn ritual drama.

In the fourteenth century, *sarugaku* was also performed in the context of rural rituals, from which it also took influences. From the eighth century, government in Japan had shifted from centralized control of the land to a manorial system. Powerful aristocrats worshipped their own ancestral deities and built shrines dedicated to them in their domains as a symbol of their authority. Farm workers became clansmen of that shrine, and organized groups called *miya za* (lit. "shrine troupes"), which were entrusted with the management of the land and the running of shrine festivals. This system gradually developed from the eleventh century onwards. *Sarugaku* was performed at village festivals with strong ties to these centers as a way to pray for a good harvest. In addition, rituals usually performed in the capital were imitated and added to local festivals. This led to the multiplication of *sarugaku* troupes (*za*) in different parts of the country.

As an example, Kasuga myōjin is the clan deity of the Fujiwara, an aristocratic family that owned numerous manors and wielded power as an external relative of the emperor.[4] Their main shrine is located in Nara (in the province formerly known as Yamato), where the famous Kasuga Wakamiya Onmatsuri is held, a festival that began in the twelfth century and has continued to the present. In the vast domains of the Fujiwara clan, each territory had a shrine dedicated to the Kasuga deity, where festivals were held in a manner similar to that of the Kasuga Wakamiya in Nara. Various performing arts, including *kagura*, *bugaku*, *dengaku*, and *sarugaku*, were dedicated to the Kasuga deity. The so-called four Yamato *sarugaku* troupes (Enman'i, Yūzaki, Sakado, and Tobi) were among those that had the responsibility to perform at the Kasuga Wakamiya Onmatsuri. During the Muromachi period (1336–1573), they eventually transformed into the Konparu, Kanze, Kongō, and Hōshō troupes, respectively, which later developed into the present-day nō schools (*ryūgi*). Some actors had the honor of being given titles. For example, *tayū* was originally the name of an official position or rank, usually the fifth rank, the lowest. It was an honor for local warriors, priests, and actors to be appointed *tayū*. This title later became commonly used for *sarugaku* troupe leaders, who were then called Konparu-dayū, Kanze-dayū, and so on, after the name of their troupe.

Okina

Sarugaku troupes performing at the Kasuga Festival were divided into two groups: the "Okina group," which was responsible for the sacred performance known as *Okina*, and the "nō group," which was in charge of the dramatic pieces known as nō. *Okina* remains the oldest and most religious play in the nō repertory. In the early modern period, the dances performed in *Okina* were imported into several other performing arts, such as bunraku, kabuki, and nihon buyō, and are still performed at New Year and on special festive occasions. This performance has no complex plot; the characters of Senzai, Okina, and Sanbasō dance and pray for long life, a bountiful harvest, and peace.

Until the Edo period (1603–1868), a special shrine license was required to perform *Okina*. Even today, some actors who take on the role of Okina continue to follow pre-performance rituals, including abstaining from meals prepared by women the day before the performance and doing morning ablutions with cold water. In the "mirror room" backstage, a lacquered box containing the Okina and Sanbasō masks is placed on an altar with offerings of salt, raw rice, and sake. Here, the performers undergo a purification ritual: They eat a piece of salt and rice and drink sacred sake. These masks are considered to be *goshintai* (lit. "body of the god"), meaning that a deity is thought to reside in them. Then a flintstone is used to create sparks on the actors and on the stage—a symbolic purification by fire. The five-colored curtain rises, and a young actor solemnly carries the mask box onto the stage, followed by the other performers. In silence, the actor performing Okina steps to the front of the stage and bows deeply. The distinctive, up-tempo musical accompaniment begins, uniquely featuring three shoulder drums (*kotsuzumi*), and the Okina actor starts to sing syllables with obscure meanings, akin to a magic formula, while the chorus chants lyrics about the beauty of nature and gratitude for the deity's blessings. The actor dons the Okina mask on stage, highlighting his transition into a vehicle through which the deity can temporarily manifest itself on stage. Next, the dance of Senzai purifies the stage with vigorous shouts and foot stamps.

The "dance" of Okina consists of the actor walking across the stage following a triangular trajectory, with each vertex symbolizing a metaphysical concept: heaven, earth, and man. This section ends with a prayer for a good harvest and peace. The actor then moves to the corner, removes his mask, bows deeply once more, and leaves the stage. In the following section, a kyōgen actor in the role of Sanbasō performs an energetic dance called *momi-no-dan*, characterized by lively jumping and stomping. The third part begins with the mask bearer inviting Sanbasō to perform a dance celebrating long life. Wearing the black Sanbasō mask and holding bells, he shakes them toward the stage, symbolizing the planting of rice seeds, in the section called *suzu no dan*.

Developments

Kan'ami and Zeami

The nō plays performed after *Okina* were originally rooted in Buddhist discourse. Unfortunately, our knowledge of these plays is limited to their titles and the names of the actors as recorded in documents from the late Kamakura period (1185–1333), from which it can be inferred that their structure revolved around the depiction of miracles performed by gods or Buddhas. *Nō* was performed not only by *sarugaku* troupes but also by actors of *dengaku*, another popular performing art, and by priestesses and priests.[5]

From the end of the Kamakura period through the era of the Northern and Southern dynasties (1336–1392), some politicians found pleasure in viewing popular art forms such as *dengaku* and *sarugaku*. During these turbulent times, marked by the simultaneous reigns of two emperors, the third Ashikaga shogun Yoshimitsu (1358–1408) expressed his desire to attend a *kanjin sarugaku* performance. The word *kanjin* refers to fundraising events where part of the profits were used to restore or reconstruct buildings such as shrines or temples. This event took place at Imagumano Shrine in Kyoto in 1374 or 1375. Yoshimitsu's interest was particularly piqued by Kan'ami, a renowned actor of the Yūzaki troupe (later known as the Kanze troupe), known for their performances of *Okina* at Kasuga Shrine in Nara.[6] At the request of the shogun,

Kan'ami performed *Okina,* a role that would normally be performed by the eldest member of the *Okina* group. This was a turning point in the development of nō.

Kan'ami was known for his extraordinary abilities in mimetic performance. Zeami recalled that although his father was a tall and lanky man, he could convincingly appear as an adolescent boy or a slender woman, depending on the role.[7] The nō plays *Jinen koji*, *Hyakuman*, *Kayoi Komachi*, and *Sotoba Komachi* are among the nō attributed to Kan'ami that are still performed today. His plays are generally based on dialogue, and song and dance are not used as abstract means of expression but appear only in scenes where a character is actually performing them. Some of the characters in these plays are ordinary people, although they may be portrayed in a heightened emotional state. While these plays often have a Buddhist background, they do not depict supernatural events such as miracles or apparitions. For example, in *Jinen koji* the protagonist is a lay priest who performs various songs and dances to rescue a child kidnapped by slave traders. Similarly, in *Hyakuman* a mother driven to madness in her desperate search for her lost son is eventually reunited with him after dancing and singing in a temple during a Buddhist ritual.

Kan'ami initiated a process of developing nō that distanced it from the previous forms. Among the innovations for which he was recognized by the public was the incorporation of a pre-existing style of chanted narrative called *kusemai* into nō. *Kusemai* was a form of song narrative popular at the time that emphasized rhythmic enunciation, performed by women who specialized in this artform.[8] In one of his treatises, Zeami claims that his father Kan'ami learned the art of *kusemai* from a professional female performer.[9] The term *kuse*, used in nō to refer to a specific segment (*shōdan*) within a play, is believed to be a derivative of *kusemai*. These innovations, though gradual, resulted in a substantial transformation of nō from what was predominantly dialogue-driven drama into a form of musical drama.

Another notable event occurred when shogun Ashikaga Yoshimitsu attended the *sarugaku* performance at the Imagumano Shrine in Kyoto. Zeami was about 12 years old when he captivated the 17-year-old Yoshimitsu with his talent and beauty. As a result, Yoshimitsu took Zeami with him to his residence, where the young performer started serving as an attendant. As Zeami spent time at the shogun's court, he was exposed to a mixture of sophisticated cultural influences from both the court nobility and the emerging samurai class. These included various art forms and literary traditions such as *waka* (classical poetry), *renga* (linked verse), and other forms of secular and religious literature.[10]

Zeami soon realized the importance of the relationship between the new aristocratic patrons and his art. This was a second crucial turning point in the history of nō. Zeami utilized the numerous commentaries on literary works available at that time to craft plays that appealed to the aristocratic class through their rich literary content. Drawing from the techniques of *waka* and *renga*, he ensured these plays were also infused with the aesthetic quality of *yūgen* to meet the refined tastes of his audience. The term *yūgen*, often associated with the aesthetics of nō, has different connotations depending on the period, but it can generally be translated as "profound elegance."[11]

After the death of his patron Yoshimitsu, Zeami lost his position as a favorite performer to *dengaku*, which was sponsored by the fourth shogun Yoshimochi (1386–1428). From then on, Zeami focused on writing. Zeami is probably the first *sarugaku* actor to receive a rich education, with private lessons from one of the most important literary figures of his time, poet and courtier Nijō Yoshimoto (1320–1388). No written documents by playwrights or actors before this time have been discovered, suggesting that they had very low literacy. However, Zeami left a wealth of documents, including numerous plays and what came to be called "treatises," twenty-three memoirs in which he wrote instructions on his art, advice to his descendants, and comments on other performers. They are known as Japan's oldest books on theatre theory, but their circulation was limited to a select group of performers, and they were passed on only within actor families until they were "rediscovered" and first published in 1905.[12]

In his treatises, Zeami discusses nō using terms such as *kokoro*, an elusive word that literally means "heart," "mind," or "soul," probably referring to the knowledge, emotion, and will through which the role and script should be expressed. A successful performance should result in *hana*, literally "flower," referring to something exciting, unusual, or new to the audience. Zeami noted that, to realize this ideal, it is essential to make a constant effort to educate oneself throughout life. Additionally, it is important to perform in a manner that aligns with one's age, while always maintaining a fresh perspective on the art. Zeami also believed that performers should avoid roles that did not match their physical appearance. For example, an old actor should not try to realistically imitate a young girl.[13]

In his writings, Zeami analyzes the portrayal of demons in Yamato *sarugaku*. He argues that instead of embodying fierce-looking demons (a style he called *rikidōfū*), performers should opt for a more nuanced approach characterized by a gentle power without excessive physical exertion (*saidōfū*). This approach, according to Zeami, is preferable because it acknowledges that these characters, despite their demonic appearance, have a fundamentally human heart. This added psychological depth to what would otherwise be two-dimensional characters.[14] Zeami also incorporated the "Dance of the Heavenly Maiden" (*tennyo no mai*), originally performed by the renowned actor Inuō of the rival Ōmi sarugaku troupe, into his repertory (Figure 3). Inuō, who had already won the admiration of the shogun before Zeami's era, was celebrated for this graceful dance. Zeami favored works with women and young noble men as protagonists to represent the "flower" of the ethereal world favored by the aristocracy. If they danced gracefully, *yūgen* could be achieved.

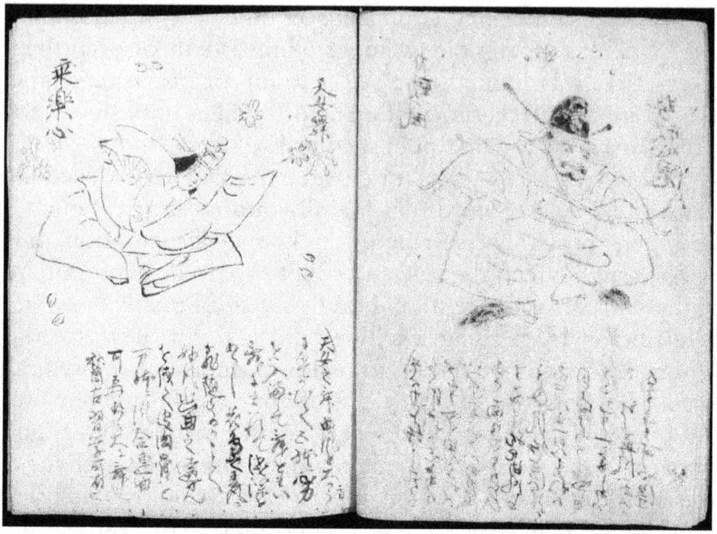

FIGURE 3 The *"Dance of the Heavenly Maiden" (left) from Zeami's* Figure Drawing of the Two Arts and the Three Modes. *On the right, the verso of "The Style of Violent Movement."* Nikyoku santai ningyōzu. *Noh Theatre Research Institute, Hōsei University.*

In the plays before this era, the characters performing dances were entertainers and deities appearing in the form of elderly men, but Zeami gradually expanded this range to include heavenly maidens, young and powerful male deities, female deities, and plays in which other kinds of human characters expressed themselves through dance. The emphasis on dance is one of Zeami's most important contributions to the renewal of the art.[15]

Zeami also showed a preference for plots in which the protagonists are ghosts who appear in the present to tell stories about their past lives. When this happens, the narrative time and space seem to warp, intertwining the past with the present. This plot structure was later called *mugen nō*. *Mugen* is a term that reflects the Buddhist view of life, depicting it as transient and fleeting as a dream, and urging the release of all attachments (see Chapter 2, *Mugen nō* and *genzai nō*). This plot format is not Zeami's creation, but rather a formulation based on Buddhist discourse that illustrates how Buddha's teachings have the power to lead a lost soul to enlightenment. Zeami presents *mugen nō* as an ideal medium for adapting tales from classical literature for his contemporaries. For example, it is possible that previously ghosts of warriors would have been depicted as venting their resentment in their descent into hell. However, through the use of *mugen nō*, Zeami created plays in which Taira clan warriors, more inclined toward poetry and music than warfare, reminisce about a life of elegance and express deep sorrow over dying in battle.

At that time, the most prestigious position in *sarugaku* was that of the *gakutōshiki* (director of music and dance), who oversaw the rituals at shrines. Zeami reached the pinnacle of his career when he was appointed *gakutōshiki* at the politically influential Daigoji Kiyotaki shrine in Kyoto in 1424. Although Zeami and *sarugaku* actors were still expected to attend banquets with the nobility and entertain them with dancing and singing, presiding over the performing arts dedicated to the gods as *gakutōshiki* allowed them take pride in the fact that *sarugaku* was a sacred performance. Indeed, Zeami's plays have a strong entertainment aspect, but he was keenly aware that the origin of their drama was a dedication to the gods, and he was proud of the origin of this artform. To understand this further, it is instructive to examine the history of *sarugaku* as discussed by Zeami in his treatises, particularly in Section 4 (Divine Purport) of *Fūshi kaden* (*Transmitting the Flower through Effects and Attitudes*, 1400 to around 1418).[16]

The origins of Japanese performing arts can be traced back to the myth of the Heavenly Cave, in which the sun goddess Amaterasu retreated into a cave and plunged the world into darkness. She was lured out by the dance of the goddess Uzume, and with Amaterasu's reappearance, light returned to the universe. Zeami also traces the beginnings of *sarugaku* to India. He recounts how, in order to pacify the outcasts who were disrupting the Buddha's sermon, one disciple played the flute and drums behind the Buddha, while another disciple performed sixty-six plays. Mesmerized by these performances, the outcasts were silenced, allowing the Buddha to continue. Zeami identifies these sixty-six plays as the fundamental elements of *sarugaku*.

In addition, Zeami tells the story of the historical figure Hada no Kawakatsu, who was originally from Korea but immigrated to Japan and served five emperors. According to legend, he was born in a jar that washed up in the flooded Hase River in Nara,[17] and later claimed to be the reincarnation of the Chinese emperor Qin Shi Huang. Because of his subsequent success at the imperial court, he was given the surname Qin 秦 (pronounced Hada in Japanese) by the Japanese emperor. During the reign of the 33rd Empress Suiko (593–628), Prince Shōtoku commissioned Kawakatsu to revive sixty-six plays based on Indian legends to restore peace in times of disaster. Prince Shōtoku defined the sixty-six plays as 申楽 (*sarugaku*), an abbreviated version of 神楽 (*kagura*, meaning music and dance for the gods). The reason for this was that "申" means "to dedicate," signifying that people would offer performances to the gods, sharing with them this entertainment. However, the kanji character "申" is also associated with the monkey in the Chinese zodiac, so it was decided to call this artform *sarugaku*.

Legend has it that after passing his art on to his descendants, Kawakatsu disappeared aboard a wooden boat to prevent his body from being displayed. When the boat was found, the remains were distorted into an inhuman form and began to haunt people. In an attempt to appease its spirit, people worshipped it as a deity. Zeami explains that this deity became known as Ōsake myōjin (meaning "Great Savage God") and is the Japanese equivalent of the Indian deity Bishamonten. Later, in the *Heian* period, the 62nd emperor Murakami (946–967) ordered Ujiyasu, a descendant of Kawakatsu, to perform the sixty-six plays in the palace as a prayer. His brother-in-law, who performed with Ujiyasu at that time, is considered to be the ancestor of the Konparu school. Later, because the sixty-six plays were too many to be performed in a single day, only three plays were chosen. These became the three parts of *Okina*.

This story presented by Zeami was rooted in a sense of pride in being part of the family responsible for the religious rituals. Emphasizing their ancestry as descendants of individuals who offered prayers for the peace of the nation, conversely, seems to suggest that nō had become more of an entertainment rather than a solemn ritual.[18]

In 1424, two years before Zeami assumed the position of *gakutōshiki* at Daigoji Kiyotaki Shrine, he had already entered the priesthood and had passed over leadership of the Kanze troupe to his son Jūrō Motomasa (?–1432). Before Motomasa was born, Zeami had adopted his nephew Saburō Motoshige, known as On'ami (1398–1467), as his heir. On'ami had already won the favor of Yoshimochi's younger brother, Gien (later known as the sixth shogun, Yoshinori), who was the ruler of another important Kyoto temple, Shōren'in. Because Zeami wanted his biological son to inherit the Kanze troupe, he refrained from passing the leadership to On'ami. As a result, the Kanze troupe split into two factions, with Zeami delaying his retirement to support Motomasa.

Motomasa remains a somewhat mysterious figure. Only a few pieces have been attributed to him, and some of them differ markedly from Zeami's artistic style. Instead, they are closer to the style of his grandfather, Kan'ami. For example, Motomasa set the play *Sumidagawa* in his own time, rather than using the historical court tales favored by Zeami. At the end of the story, the mother sees an apparition of her son, but when she reaches out to embrace him, the vision disappears. This somber moment contrasts sharply with the typically happy endings that Zeami favored in the final scenes of his plays. Apparently, Motomasa insisted on using a child actor to portray the appearance of the son's ghost, while Zeami insisted that this was not necessary.[19] This divergence in their artistic sensibilities adds a fascinating dimension to the relationship between father and son. The works attributed to Motomasa that are still performed today are *Yoroboshi*, *Utaura*, *Morihisa*, *Tomonaga*, and *Sumidagawa*.

After the succession of Yoshimochi's younger brother, Ashikaga Yoshinori (1394–1441), as the sixth shogun in 1429, the Kanze troupe received a lukewarm reception. Later, in 1430, Yoshinori stripped Zeami of his role as *gakutōshiki* at the Daigoji Kiyotaki shrine, a position that was subsequently given to On'ami, who excelled at performing the more powerful demon nō plays, a style favored by Yoshinori. Records show that 71 percent of On'ami's forty-five recorded nō performances fell into categories four and five (see Chapter 2, Repertory and categorization). This indicates a preference for dynamic characters and performances, in contrast to Zeami's more subtle approach.[20] Perhaps influenced by this adverse situation, Zeami's other son, Motoyoshi (dates unknown), gave up his acting career. As evidence of his dedicated nō training, Motoyoshi bequeathed to his father the writings he had long been recording from his father Zeami's words. He then became a monk. This collection of writings is known today as *Sarugaku Dangi* (Talks on Sarugaku, 1430).

Tragedy struck again in 1432, when Zeami's eldest son, Motomasa, died prematurely in his early 40s while traveling to a performance. The profound despair of his 70-year-old father, Zeami, is poignantly captured in the document entitled *Museki isshi* (*Traces of a Dream on a Single Sheet*, 1432).[21] Despite these challenges, shogun Yoshinori's mistreatment of Zeami continued, leading to Zeami's exile to Sado Island, far from the capital. It remains unclear whether Zeami was eventually pardoned and returned to the capital, or if he died on the island. The last known record of him is a short letter entitled *Kintōsho* (*The Golden Isle*, 1432), which he wrote in Sado and sent to his son-in-law, Konparu Ujinobu Zenchiku (1405–1470?), who was the *tayū* of the Konparu troupe.

Zeami's twenty-three treatises, which have undergone numerous revisions, remain a subject of fascination for scholars, who continue to propose various theories about this revision process. It is widely believed that in his later years Zeami devoted himself to theorizing about how to perfect his art in a way that would resonate with audiences. After his ordination as a Zen monk, Zeami's immersion in Zen philosophy profoundly influenced his philosophical perspective. Initially, he posited the notion of the "flower" that resides even in an aged body.[22] In his later years he developed the notion that an experienced artist, having fully mastered his techniques, reaches a level of performance that appears effortless, resembling the simplicity of a novice's expression. However, this appearance belies a deeper mastery, far surpassing the beginner's initial attempts at outer form. Zeami recognized that only a highly discerning audience would be able to appreciate this subtlety.[23] He may have found it frustrating that many, including Yoshinori and his associates, failed to grasp the true essence of his artistry. Scholars continue to debate the authorship and date of Zeami's works. Of the approximately 240 surviving pieces, about 50 are attributed to him, many of which follow the *mugen nō* format.

After Zeami

Zeami's concept of *mugen nō* was transmitted and refined by his son-in-law Konparu Zenchiku. Under Zenchiku, the interpretation of nō dance became more conceptual, moving away from human drama to express more abstract concepts, such as the depiction of anguish and the reenactment of memories. In early plays, characters performed a dance only when justified by the narrative, and they were typically depicted as performers within the story. Over time, however, plays began to feature song and dance as a non-mimetic expression of a character's feelings, without the need for narrative justification. Similar to Zeami, Zenchiku left behind several treatises. These works offer detailed information on the theory of performance, incorporating elements of Shintoism and Buddhism. Scholars continue to study them and offer new interpretations.[24] Plays attributed to him include *Bashō*, *Nonomiya*, *Teika*, *Tamakazura*, *Ugetsu*, and *Matsumushi*.[25]

While Zenchiku immersed himself in this artistic endeavor, significant social changes were unfolding around him. The shogunate was rocked by recurring succession disputes that weakened its authority. In 1441, during a performance by On'ami, a regional lord named Akamatsu assassinated shogun Yoshinori. After this, emerging warrior factions from various regions began to engage in territorial disputes with their neighboring domains, rendering the role of the shogunate largely symbolic. The proceeds from land taxes, originally centralized under the control of authorities such as temples and shrines, became increasingly difficult to collect. This led to the empowerment of local warrior factions to administer them.

As the country entered what is now known as the Warring States period (late fifteenth to late sixteenth centuries) there was a notable shift in social dynamics. The wider population began to wield more influence, and a trend toward meritocracy among lower-ranking warriors reshaped the cultural landscape. Small cultural salon groups emerged, gathering in intimate settings to participate in activities such as tea ceremonies, flower arranging, incense appreciation, and linked verse poetry. Rather than performing full plays, participants of these salons staged short dances and chant excerpts in a manner similar to modern karaoke. While these short performances had been enjoyed as entertainment during Zeami's time, they evolved into a refined cultural pursuit during this era.

New plays continued to be written, contributing significantly to the repertory that has survived to the present day. Zenchiku's grandson, Konparu Zenpō (1454–?), composed notable works such as *Ikkaku sennin* and *Ikuta Atsumori*. In addition, Kanze Kojirō Nobumitsu (1451 or 1452–1516), On'ami's seventh son, wrote *Funa Benkei*, *Momijigari*, *Rashōmon*, and *Chōryō*. Nobumitsu's son, Kanze Yajirō Nagatoshi (1488–1541), composed plays such as *Rinzō*, *Enoshima*, and *Shōzon*. These works, characterized by their musical and lyrical elements with lighter and more exotic themes, marked a departure from the gravity and solemnity of Zeami and Zenchiku's creations, and played a pivotal role in the continued evolution and diversification of nō during a period of significant social and cultural change.

While plays continued to feature religious allegories, authors of this period began to weave in tales of bravery linked to individual ancestors and tales of revenge that inspired courage. This era saw a preference for flashy, spectacular, and showy productions known as *furyū nō*. For example, *Tsuchigumo* (*The Ground Spider*) is based on an episode in *The Tale of the Heike*, which centers on the legendary warrior Minamoto no Yorimitsu, who is suffering from a mysterious illness. A strange-looking monk visits the Yorimitsu and suddenly attacks him with cobwebs. When Yorimitsu strikes back, the monk is revealed to be a monstrous spider in disguise. The warrior's henchman then follows the spider's blood trail to its lair. The play climaxes with an exciting battle in which paper streamers simulate spider webs. The monster is finally defeated. In *Sesshōseki* (*The Killing Stone*), a massive stone is the central set piece. According to folklore, this cursed stone kills any bird that flies over it. The stone traps the spirit of a nine-tailed fox, a malevolent female entity from ancient India responsible for deceiving a Chinese king and causing the downfall of his kingdom. When a monk prays to the stone, it breaks in two, revealing the spirit fox. The play ends with the exorcism of the fox's spirit through prayer.

Featuring heroic battles against evil entities and thrilling stage effects, these plays can be compared to the contemporary superhero narratives of action films. In contrast to Zeami's intricate portrayals of inner struggle, the plays of this period, which eschewed deep psychological exploration, marked a return to the foundational themes of nō that predated Zeami, focusing on didactic narratives deeply rooted in Buddhist teachings.

Nō as leisure

As nō grew in popularity, other forms emerged that allowed people to enjoy aspects of nō in different ways. One such form was *ko-utai* (short *utai*), which were abridged chants consisting of famous key passages taken from nō performances. These *ko-utai* were included in the popular song collection *Kanginshū* (1518), indicating that these sections had spread as a cultural phenomenon enjoyed by middle-class townspeople. This was seen in the emergence of *renza* and *yose*—gatherings where people of different social status enjoyed various forms of entertainment including nō, tea, flower arranging, incense, poetry readings, and so on—along with increased social mobility (a phenomenon called *gekokujō*). In the midst of this social change, what had been associated with "high culture" began to shift from the ruling elite to ordinary citizens. This change gave rise to amateur nō performers known as *tesarugaku*, whose shows gained considerable popularity.[26] These amateur performers often demonstrated ability, popularity, and energy that rivaled and sometimes surpassed that of their official counterparts. Notable *tesarugaku* performers included Shimotsuma Shōshin (1551–1616), a priest at the influential Honganji temple in Kyoto, and wealthy merchants such as Toraya, as well as female nō performers.[27] The first record of female *sarugaku* performances dates back to 1432 in Toba, Kyoto, where five beautiful women performed at a fundraising nō event. This performance gained considerable fame, and later that same month, the women were invited to perform at the shogun's residence, where they received a reward.[28] Subsequently, female *sarugaku* seemed to have become popular, as several documents from that period suggest. The women's beautiful appearances and voices were praised, and the novelty of women performing arts traditionally done by men likely played a role in their popularity. The *sarugaku* performed by women transcended mere imitation of male *sarugaku* and contributed to the creation of new theatrical forms, such as kabuki.[29] These practitioners enjoyed the freedom to interpret and perform nō in their own unique styles, and also contributed to the art form by sharing their knowledge and skills.

During this period, nō professionals performed a variety of duties. They often accompanied their patron warriors to the battlefields, providing entertainment amid the turmoil of warfare. Warriors who valued both literary and martial arts hosted cultural salons where they actively participated in nō, preferring to dance and chant themselves rather than be mere spectators. Professional nō performers thus assumed the role of instructors, meticulously teaching their art. Among the *tesarugaku* performers, those with exceptional talents also became teachers. Each of these individuals directed and performed nō with their unique interpretations. Even the professional instructors were sometimes supplanted by *tesarugaku* performers who taught a variety of arts, perhaps in a more accessible and affordable manner.

Beginning in the late Muromachi period, the growing involvement of amateurs in nō led to an increased demand for written texts. Previously, trained professionals had relied on oral and corporeal transmission, with Zeami's manuscripts being among the few scripts available. However, teaching nō to amateurs such as samurai and influential townspeople required the support of texts. Manuals began to be written, documenting instructors' teachings on the knowledge, mindset, and physical techniques required for nō. In addition, structured teaching systems based on levels of difficulty and stages of learning were established, complete with certificates for mastering each stage. This later evolved into the "license system" (*menjō seido*) still in use today. Instructors began to document secret techniques on paper to deepen the bond with their students, often in exchange for money. Choreographic sections were segmented and named, with detailed instructions for actions such as stepping or turning at specific moments, leading to the creation of *kata* (formalized movement sequences). Nō had already begun a process of transformation into a classical performing art.

The Warring States period was characterized by prolonged warfare, and also by the rise of *daimyō*, the regional warlords who sought to consolidate fragmented territories under their rule in order to achieve national dominance. Many *daimyō* were also passionate supporters of nō, appreciating its cultural value. Nō performers, celebrated for their artistry, received compensation for teaching their skills and revealing secret techniques. This practice of providing financial support to performers, which began before the times of Kan'ami and Zeami, gained momentum as nō found favor with the influential figures of the era. In addition to their performance fees, nō performers were often given material gifts and occasionally land. The practice of rewarding these performers, signifying both their esteemed status and their critical social role, became particularly prominent during these turbulent times.

Oda Nobunaga (1534–1582), a key figure in the Warring States period who failed to realize his goal of national unification, showed a preference for *kōwaka mai* (a form of narrative performance) over nō. Nevertheless, he held the leader of the Umewaka *sarugaku* troupe from Tamba province in high esteem and, like many warlords of his time, rewarded his favorite *sarugaku* performers with territories. His successor, Toyotomi Hideyoshi (1537–1598), who rose from humble beginnings to become the unifier of the country, developed a deep affection for nō after turning 60 and assuming leadership of the country. Hideyoshi sponsored the creation of new nō plays that celebrated his own achievements, such as *Yoshino mōde* (*A Pilgrimage to Mt. Yoshino*), *Kōyasan mōde* (*A Pilgrimage to Mt. Kōya*), *Akechi uchi* (*The Attack on Akechi*), *Shibata*, and *Hōjō*. Hideyoshi went so far as to portray himself in these plays. He mainly supported actors from the Konparu and *tesarugaku* troupes.

An important development affecting *sarugaku* was Hideyoshi's *haitō mai* system, which involved the distribution of rice to *sarugaku* performers of the four troupes (Kanze, Hōshō, Konparu, Kongō) that operated in the Yamato region. This system allocated a portion of the *daimyō*'s annual tribute to the shogunate as a stipend for nō actors. According to the *Kanze za shihai no koto* (*Matters Concerning the Governance of the Kanze Troupe*), a document issued by Toyotomi Hideyoshi in 1597, 955 *koku* (a unit of rice sufficient for one person's annual consumption) were allotted to the Kanze troupe, effectively supporting some 955 individuals from important performer families and their associates.

This led to smaller *sarugaku* groups (also known as *gunsho sarugaku za*) being absorbed into the more prominent Yamato *sarugaku* groups. Some of these smaller groups still exist today within various nō schools as influential kinship groups, such as the Umewaka and Yamashina families of the Kanze school. This system was largely maintained by Tokugawa Ieyasu (1543–1616), who succeeded Hideyoshi. In addition, Hideyoshi's nephew Hidetsugu (1568–1595) commissioned the creation of *Utai shō*, a document collecting annotated nō texts by monks from the Gozan temples and others. By this time, the language used in nō had become archaic and sophisticated, differing significantly from common speech.

Expansion and formalization

Nō and official celebrations of the Edo shogunate

Tokugawa Ieyasu betrayed Toyotomi Hideyoshi by sidestepping the unification of the country following the Siege of Osaka (1614–1615), strategically choosing to develop the wild lands to the east, leading to the establishment of Edo (Tokyo) as his political center. This pivotal decision heralded the beginning of the Edo period, which spanned two centuries from 1603 to 1868. Tokugawa remained in Kyoto to receive the title of *Seii taishogun* (Great General Who Subdues the Barbarians) from the emperor in 1603 and organized a three-day nō performance to celebrate the proclamation. A total of thirty-two nō plays were performed at the event, which was attended by prominent political figures.

Ieyasu's decision to have nō performed on the occasion of official rituals organized by the Edo shogunate was based on several factors. His personal familiarity with and appreciation for nō, acquired from Kanze actors and through his own participation in nō and kyōgen performances from an early age, likely influenced his decision. In addition, he followed the precedent set by the Muromachi shogunate, where similar celebratory nō performances were organized during shogun proclamations. For example, when Ashikaga Yoshiaki (1537–1597), the last ruler of the Muromachi period, was proclaimed shogun in 1568, a total of thirteen nō plays were performed. Ieyasu likely sought to continue this tradition to legitimize his own authority and consolidate power.

Although originally intended to entertain Oda Nobunaga, the ceremonial nō performances for Ashikaga Yoshiaki shogun's proclamation was recognized by scholars of ancient rites as symbolic celebrations of the shogunate's authority.[30] Ieyasu followed this precedent and, upon his proclamation as shogun, increased the volume of nō plays during the ceremony to exceed even historical norms. Meanwhile, Ieyasu refrained from performing nō and kyōgen himself, maintaining the dignity befitting his position.[31] With its formal adoption as the official ritual of the warrior class, nō began to be influenced by warrior etiquette, martial arts, and the spiritual ethos of the samurai, further solidifying its importance during the Edo period.

Patronage, politics, and regulations

To consolidate the hereditary succession of the shogunate within his immediate family, Ieyasu relinquished the shogunate to his eldest son, Hidetada (1579–1632), and retired. While Ieyasu had inherited Hideyoshi's *haitō mai* system for maintaining the four Yamato *sarugaku* troupes,

Ieyasu was unable to make any political arrangements to control nō during his brief two-year tenure as shogun. In contrast to Ieyasu, both his son Hidetada and Hidetada's son Iemitsu (1604–1651) openly expressed their preference for nō by attending performances.

A key symbolic gesture was Hidetada's appointment of Kita Shichi-dayū (1586–1653) to a prominent position. Born into a family of ophthalmologists in Sakai, Osaka, he started to perform at the age of 7, thus earning fame as *Shichi-dayū* (literally, "seven-year-old top performer"). Between the ages of 9 and 10 he joined the Kongō troupe, whose head, Kongō-dayū (Yaichi, d. 1605), adopted him because of his exceptional talent. At the age of 14 or 16, Shichi-dayū took the name Kongō Saburō. In 1605, after Yaichi's death, Saburō was forced to retire due to his past association with the Toyotomi faction during the Battle of Osaka. He then turned to teaching nō to female entertainers in Kyoto's pleasure districts. At the behest of Tokugawa Ieyasu, Yaichi's son Ukyō succeeded him as Kongō-dayū. However, in 1619, after Ieyasu's retirement, Saburō, then 34 years old, was summoned to Edo by the new shogun, Hidetada, to perform at a *kanjin* event the following year.

Kanjin nō, originally organized as a charitable event to raise funds for the restoration of temples and shrines, became a customary event held by *tayū* in Edo. In Saburō's case, he did not assume the title of Kongō-dayū but was allowed to give performances under the patronage of the shogun. With continued support from the shogunate, he changed his name to Kita Shichi-dayū in 1627 and founded the independent Kita school. Following a shogunate decision, 200 *koku* of rice, out of the 300 *koku* originally allocated to Kongō-dayū, was now to go to Shichi-dayū.

The emergence of the Kita school was met with harsh criticism. In 1634, when Shichi-dayū performed *Sekidera Komachi*, a particularly revered play, he was strongly criticized for what was considered poor acting. As a result, he was placed under house arrest until he was pardoned the following year.

Despite his conviction, Shichi-dayū was reinstated early at the request of the powerful *daimyō* Date Masamune (1567–1636). The shogunate intervened to ensure that all four *tayū* and their sons studied under Shichi-dayū, but the Konparu family, the oldest of the four schools, under the sixty-fifth *tayū* of the Konparu troupe, Hachirō Motonobu, initially resisted. In 1647 the shogunate issued an order forcing compliance. After a nō performance in August 1651 to celebrate the proclamation of the fourth Tokugawa shogun (Ietsuna, 1641–1680), Shichi-dayū retired. His fourth son, Masayoshi (1624–1665), succeeded him as head of the Kita school. The special treatment accorded the Kita school by the shogun for two generations arguably resulted from its artistic appeal.

The rise of Kita Shichi-dayū became a significant event, sparking debates among the townspeople about the Kita school's artistry. As reflected in the book *Bushō goma*, critics claimed that Shichi-dayū's nō was disorderly and deviated from tradition. In response, another book, *Sarugutsuwa*, was published, which defended the art of the Kita school.[32] While the Kita school was appreciated by lovers of novelty, it was considered an outlier by those who valued tradition. Masayoshi is thought to have met a tragic end, murdered after a nō performance at Edo Castle.

Tokugawa Ietsuna took office two years after Shichi-dayū's death in 1653. Within the warrior elite, nō dance and song developed into a refined art form. It was used not only to curry favor with the shogun but also to cultivate the physical and mental prowess of the samurai. Despite the benefits of practicing these arts, Chief Minister Sakai Tadakatsu (1587–1662) expressed displeasure with warriors investing their time in nō, saying that "doing *sarugaku* does not make one a samurai."[33] However, he acknowledged the suitability of nō as a ceremonial art.

Tadakatsu's successor, Sakai Tadakiyo (1624–1681), arranged for the four official troupes to participate in the 500-year-old rituals at Kōfukuji Temple and the Kasuga Shrine in Nara, allowing the performers to devote more attention to their engagements at Edo Castle. The Kanze troupe was granted an exemption, while two from the remaining Konparu, Kongō, and Hōshō troupes were required to routinely perform in Nara—the shogunate covered their expenses. The non-participating troupes were instead required to attend the New Year's ceremony hosted by the shogun, emphasizing their connection to the Edo shogunate rather than to the Kasuga Shrine or the Kōfukuji Temple. In addition, the number of official performances at Honmaru Palace in Edo Castle, known as *omote nō*, was limited to five plays per event. Furthermore, in 1668 actors were forbidden to carry swords, clearly distinguishing them from the warrior elite.

However, these efforts to impose restrictions ultimately proved futile. The next shogun, Tsunayoshi (1646–1709), showed an even greater interest in nō. When he was lord of the Tatebayashi domain (now Gunma Prefecture), like many other feudal lords he was enthusiastic about performing nō himself. Six or seven nō plays were performed to commemorate the proclamation of the shogun's succession, disregarding the rule that stipulated a maximum of five plays per event and prohibiting nō actors not officially employed by the government from performing on such official occasions.[34]

Tsunayoshi's enduring love for nō, especially for the Hōshō school style he had favored since his days as the Tatebayashi *daimyō*, changed the way feudal lords viewed these actors. An active participant in nō performances himself, Tsunayoshi enjoyed sharing nō and encouraging its performance among *daimyō* and their retainers. This widespread support led to a proliferation of nō performances, which were extensively documented both in the capital and in various domains, sometimes exceeding the capacity of official records to capture them all. Tsunayoshi went so far as to banish or transfer actors he did not like. For example, when *kotsuzumi* player Kanze Shinkurō VI (1636–1688) was asked to perform *Dōjōji* with the head of the Hōshō troupe, he refused, claiming that it was technically impossible due to differences in performance style.[35] Tsunayoshi banished him and forced him to transfer to the Hōshō group, where he refused to play.[36] On the other hand, shogun Tsunayoshi's favored actors were promoted to lower-ranking samurai positions.[37]

During this period, it was not uncommon for both nō actors and feudal lords to perform rare plays for the pleasure of the shogun. For instance, Zeami's holograph of one of today's most popular plays, *Yoroboshi* (originally composed by Motomasa) was discovered in 1941, but the plot it contained turned out to be quite different from the one that was performed at the time and is still performed today. It seems that its present form was reconstructed during a period of increased interest in rare plays in Tsunayoshi's reign.

Feudal lords followed the shogun's lead in favoring nō, often employing their own actors within their domains. Wealthy merchants also developed a strong interest in nō. As a result, a hierarchy began to take shape, with the official nō performers of the Edo shogunate occupying the highest position, followed by the nō performers employed by feudal lords, those who instructed merchants in nō, and finally the amateur nō enthusiasts.

The next shogun, Tokugawa Ienobu (1662–1712) was an important patron of the Kita school and, emulating Tsunayoshi, continued the tradition of granting samurai status to nō actors. This practice is highlighted in the case of the actor Manabe Akifusa (1666–1720), son of an official nō actor of the Kōfu domain (now Yamanashi Prefecture), who had a childhood association with Tokugawa Tsunatoyo (1662–1712), later known as Ienobu. Even after becoming shogun, Ienobu's support for Akifusa continued, eventually leading to Akifusa's elevation to the rank of *rōjū*, a senior advisor to the shogun.

The seventh Tokugawa shogun, Ietsugu (1709–1716), became shogun at the age of 4 and died after only four years, but his reign was supported by Akifusa and the Confucianist scholar Arai Hakuseki (1657–1725). However, both were disgraced during the reign of the eighth shogun, Tokugawa Yoshimune (1684–1751). He instituted a policy of nō control to correct the chaos caused by the previous shoguns' unbridled enthusiasm for nō and the promotion of performers into the ranks of the samurai.

Yoshimune, who was originally the lord of the Kishū domain south of Osaka, employed Tokuda Chikatada (1677–?) as an official nō actor. Documents show that Yoshimune emphasized the importance of preserving the traditional performance methods of nō, ensuring that they remained true to their historical roots.[38] This commitment to authenticity extended to his efforts to restore order to both the disorganized economy of the shogunate and the nō system. Known for his cautious demeanor, Yoshimune's principles were deeply influenced by Ieyasu's emphasis on honoring precedent. He did not relegate nō actors who had been promoted to the samurai ranks to their original status, but he did demote Manabe Akifusa to a lower samurai rank.

Yoshimune's celebratory nō performance for his own proclamation as shogun lasted five days, reverting to the precedent of five-day celebrations. Such performances at annual events in Edo Castle were overseen by an administrator, known as a *furenagashi*, who properly managed ceremonial, annual, and private nō events of the concern of the shogunate, and acted as an intermediary between the shogunate and nō performers. Of the two people appointed as *furenagashi* during Yoshimune's time, Matsui Kizaemon (dates unknown) was a kyōgen actor associated with the Konparu troupe, and Yamada Tōemon (dates unknown) was a *kotsuzumi* instrumentalist of the Kanze troupe. Their descendants also served as *furenagashi* for generations until the end of the Edo period.

In 1721 Yoshimune had each nō and kyōgen troupe submit a list of plays they could perform. This helped to establish the repertory of each troupe. The *furenagashi* was to keep a record of all performances in a document known as the *Furenagashi onō gumi* (*Nō Program administered by the* furenagashi). This document is a complete record of public and private nō performances staged or organized by the Edo shogunate between January 1721 and March 1862; there were over 1,400 performances. The canonization of the nō art form became even more pronounced during Yoshimune's reign. No new plays or revivals were permitted, and unconventional performance methods were allowed only if they could be shown to have historical precedents.

A year of nō as ritual entertainment at Edo Castle

Nō gradually became institutionalized as part of the ritual events and organization of the Edo shogunate. Here are some examples. The first was the first nō chant performance of the New Year (*utai-zome*), a tradition dating back to at least the end of the Muromachi period. Second, ceremonial nō plays were performed at various celebrations within the shogun's family, including births, coming-of-age ceremonies, marriages, promotions, and the proclamation of a new shogun. Third, nō plays were also staged after the conclusion of official ceremonies, such as visits to Momijiyama (an area within Edo Castle that housed shrines dedicated to former shoguns) or Tōshōgū, the shrine in Nikkō dedicated to Tokugawa Ieyasu, the founder of the shogunate. Finally, nō performances were arranged for visiting court nobles from Kyoto as well as Korean or Ryūkyū (now Okinawa) court dignitaries.

These four official events were called *omote nō* (official ceremonial nō) and were performed on the official nō stage (*omote butai*) in the Honmaru, the central part of Edo Castle, where the shogun conducted his political affairs. *Omote nō* events opened with *Okina*, and nō and kyōgen were performed alternately in a sequence of five plays. *Daimyō* and their retinues were required to attend this event. According to the diary of a low-ranking samurai at the end of the Edo period, when samurai acted as guards for *omote nō*, they were not allowed to move an inch, which was a painful duty because their legs became numb sitting on their knees. So, they would avoid drinking tea, and during the performance they would move their toes unnoticed, being careful not to fall over because of the numbness.[39]

The private celebrations and entertainments containing nō, commonly known as *oku nō*, consisted of events including performances intended to entertain the shogun or his family, such as the welcoming party for the married princesses of the shogun returning to Edo Castle (*nagusami nō*), and the private parties of the shogun's family (*uchi iwai*). These were held on the nō stage in the Nishinomaru, the shogun's family quarters. Not only the nō actors but also the shogun and his retainers would sing, dance, and play the musical accompaniment, sometimes also watched by the ladies of the inner palace. Precious costumes and masks that belonged to the host shogun and feudal lords were borrowed by the nō actors for their performances. Owning high-quality nō costumes and masks was a status symbol for these lords. If a performance was particularly outstanding, the nō actor might be honored by being given these prestigious items (see Chapter 3, Costumes).

The official nō actors of the shogunate not only performed *omote nō* and *oku nō* as described above but also served as singing and dancing instructors for the shogun, his sons, and other feudal lords. They had privileged access to the shogun and other central political figures, as well as insight into the private lives of the nobles. As part of their duties, they were required to take a written oath promising to teach without bias, maintain secrecy and discretion, refrain from conspiring with feudal lords and vassals, and avoid arrogance.

Kanze Motoakira's reform and the *iemoto* system

In the mid-Edo period, a significant reform of nō was undertaken by the fifteenth head of the Kanze group, Motoakira (1722–1774).[40] The reform, supported by shogunate officials, was in line with the shogunate's governance of nō. On the surface, it presented itself as a challenging endeavor to break with tradition. The main thrust was the revision of the official chant books (*utaibon*). The texts of the kyōgen and *waki* parts, which had previously been under the exclusive control of their performers, were also revised. The reform aimed to improve the integrity and coherence of the nō's presentation of classical literature. This included correcting inaccuracies in the presentation of sources, ensuring narrative coherence between the first and second acts, and eliminating *waka*-inspired poetic devices such as *kakekotoba* (words with double meanings). It also involved revising for a more rational interpretation of the story's timing and plot developments, clarifying the use of language, particularly in the correction of honorifics, and eliminating interpretations based on medieval classical views in favor of a perspective closer to that of the Japanese classical studies movement (*kokugaku*).

Changes in the text inevitably lead to changes in the staging. Choreography, costumes, and properties were redefined to fit the new chant books. The original repertory of 149 plays submitted to the shogunate by Motoakira's father, Kiyochika, was revised. This process not only renewed the existing canon but also revived discarded plays, expanding the repertory to a total of 210 plays. Some of the revisions were so extensive that they could be described as radical rewrites. For example, the play *Shironushi* underwent significant revisions, resulting in its title reverting to its original name, *Katsuragi Kamo*. This change was also due to the fact that nō plays, especially those related to myth, were being revised according to the text of the *Kojiki*, Japan's oldest extant chronicle compiled in 712, which was beginning to be studied in earnest at the time. It can be said that Motoakira was the first "artistic director" to take a "holistic" approach to nō, addressing the coherence of its various elements, including plot, direction, acting, costumes, and so on. He also wrote a new play, *Ume* (*The Plum*). In the 200-year history of the Edo period, this was the only new official play ever performed at Edo Castle.

However, Motoakira's revised chant books, published in 1765, were extremely unpopular, especially because their use was mandated not only for the Kanze troupes, which were directly under the control of the shogunate, but also for townspeople who studied as amateurs. For example, the literate Kanzawa Tokō (1710–1795), a contemporary of Motoakira, wrote: "If we simply use the old ways, the customs of the world will change, and what was once considered elegant will become vulgar."[41] Another critical issue was the perhaps overly ambitious expectation that everyone involved in nō—not only professional actors and musicians but also amateurs from all walks of life—would relearn plays they had already memorized.

Motoakira's new chant books were discontinued immediately after his death. Despite their brief existence of only nine years, this episode highlights the importance of nō during this period. The general consensus favored retaining the original text, emphasizing the importance of preserving traditional forms over making changes for the sake of interpretation or consistency. On the other hand, Motoakira's ingenious innovations in staging the plays were well received and have survived as performance variants (*kogaki*) to this day. Especially after the Meiji Restoration, the value of these innovations was reassessed, and today certain plays, such as *Uneme*, are almost always performed in their variant forms.

Motoakira's reform may have been acceptable within the confines of the small community of nō actors at Edo Castle. However, its failure was partly due to the fact that it forced ordinary people who were nō enthusiasts to conform to these changes. As noted above, from the late Muromachi period onward, the expansion of trade and industry allowed a portion of the townspeople and peasants to become more affluent and culturally sophisticated, and this included the study of nō.

Utai culture

Broadly speaking, nō performance can be divided into three elements: dance, chant, and music. In the Edo period, professional nō performers specialized in one role only, a tradition that, in part, continues to this day. For example, a flautist played only the flute, and a chorus singer sang exclusively in the chorus. Amateurs, however, could learn any of the nō arts if they had the time and money, but singing was encouraged as a central cultural activity. For example, the nō chant manual *Taihei ko-utai banbanzai* (1823), used in *terakoya* (private schools for townspeople), suggests that while it is not necessary to memorize an entire nō piece, it is advisable to learn some chant excerpts (*ko-utai*). Since the lyrics of nō plays evoke different types of moods, knowing nō chant (*utai*) was useful in the daily lives of townspeople, as nō excerpts were sung at a variety of events, such as weddings, flower-viewing banquets, funerals, and memorial services. The practice of singing *ko-utai* became an essential part of adult socializing, seamlessly integrated into the cultural fabric of everyday life, with its popularity extending beyond the cities to affluent farming communities, where nō singing became one of the few socially sanctioned recreational activities for farmers. Other documents asserted that it was good to practice nō chant because it would be useful later in life, but devoting oneself to the study of musical instruments and dance might lead to neglecting one's business and family.[42]

Indeed, there were numerous instances in which shogun and feudal lords became so engrossed in nō that they ignored their political responsibilities. This phenomenon was not limited to the ruling class; ordinary townspeople were also drawn to nō, sometimes suffering financial losses as a result. The novels *Saikaku oridome* and *Chōnin kōkenroku*, written by popular novelist Ihara Saikaku (1642–1693), depict a merchant who became so enamored of nō that he bought expensive nō costumes and eventually went bankrupt.[43] In response to these problems, the shogunate issued decrees against extravagance, including severe punishments such as confiscation of property for those who did not comply. Nevertheless, throughout the Edo period people continued to be drawn to nō, undeterred by the potential consequences.

The culture of nō chant among commoners gradually came under the control of the *iemoto* (headmaster) system. *Iemoto* (lit. "origin of the house") is a term used to describe the leader of a practice group in traditional arts such as the tea ceremony, flower arranging, or nō. In the first half of the Edo period, the nō teachers from whom the townspeople learned had no connection with the actors officially employed by the shogunate. From about the middle of the Edo period, however, contact between official actors and town teachers began to develop. Their relationship was based on the so-called "*iemoto* system," which still exists today. As will be discussed in more detail later, this system gradually developed during the Edo period, with the *tayū* of the five official troupes acting as *iemoto*. The *iemoto* typically instructs only his direct disciples (*jiki deshi*), who may then teach their own students, forming a hierarchical lineage of practitioners. This structure enables the *iemoto* to oversee the art at all levels, and their authority is enforced through a system of purchasable licenses required to access increasingly advanced knowledge. Issued directly by the *iemoto*, these licenses serve as proof of legitimate mastery of the art.[44]

Licensing systems for learning artistic practices, martial arts, and even *waka* predate the Edo period. Initially, the licensing (*denju*) was primarily a one-to-one arrangement. However, the *iemoto* system marked a significant departure from this, as it was organized into a vast hierarchical structure. Under this system, once an individual had been trained, they pledged lifelong allegiance to their master, a commitment that extended to their descendants. They also made a written vow to gods and buddhas to keep what they had learned strictly secret, promising not to reveal it to outsiders.

In the Edo period, although there was already a broad classification of ranks for the pieces taught, there may not have been a structured curriculum leading to graduation with a specific diploma. Instead, the master would select study pieces based on the student's level. This training continued throughout the student's life. Initially, there were independent masters who were not affiliated with the official actors of the shogunate who taught nō chants popular among commoners. However, starting around the middle of the Edo period, these independent chant teachers began to become disciples of the four shogunate-supported actor groups. Over time, the *iemoto* system evolved, placing official actors at the top and amateur enthusiasts at the bottom, thus formalizing a pyramidal hierarchy.

Kyoto is a prime example of this phenomenon. Here, Kan'ami and Zeami developed nō with the Muromachi aristocracy, and the culture of nō and singing spread among the townspeople. Nō did not decline even after the performers of the four troupes moved to Edo. A document called *Suutai yo yo no ato* (*Traces of Unaccompanied Nō Chant through the Ages*, 1818) describes how Kyoto's chanting culture changed under the control of the Kanze school. Hattori Morichika (1609–1673), also known as Fukuō Mohee Morichika and later as Sōha, the younger brother of Kanze-dayū IX (1566–1626, Tadachika, later known as Kokusetsu), served as a *waki* in the Fukuō school, affiliated with the Kanze troupe, under Ieyasu, Hidetada, and Iemitsu.[45] In his later years, Morichika retired and moved to Kyoto, where he began teaching *su-utai* (the singing of an entire nō play) to townspeople. This practice flourished with the support of Kyoto's wealthy merchants.

Morichika's legacy of teaching nō in Kyoto was carried on by his children and grandchildren. Among his direct students were merchants as well as actors in the service of feudal lords. One notable student of his, Ogawa Tokuyuki (dates unknown), originally a *waki* actor for the Kishū clan, shifted his focus to teaching chanting to the townspeople. Tokuyuki published *Kanze tōryū himitsu rangyoku* (1664), a book of secret chants for advanced students, without the permission of his master.[46] Morichika's adopted son, Hattori Sōseki (1660–1721), also known as Fukuō Mouemon Morinobu VII, later Sōseki, excommunicated Tokuyuki, fearing repercussions if the publication came to the attention of the Kanze-dayū. This episode exemplifies the extent to which even the culture of chanting for enjoyment among Kyoto's townspeople had come under the control of the leader of the Edo-based Kanze troupe.

Another disciple of Sōseki, Takemura Sadakatsu (dates unknown), who had also previously served as a *waki* actor for the Kishū clan, was a skilled event organizer. He established a monthly *su-utai* gathering on the twenty-second day of each month to coincide with the memorial service for his master, Morichika, and made it a regular event in Kyoto. The event was open to all, which helped spread *utai* culture. Sadakatsu later revealed what should have remained a secret between master and pupil, offending Sōseki and resulting in his excommunication.

Sōseki's anger originated from Sadakatsu's disclosure of his secret techniques. In 1702, during the reign of shogun Tsunayoshi, the thirteenth Kanze-dayū Shigeki from Edo performed at *kanjin* events in Kyoto. At these performances, disciples of Sōseki, including members of the Asano, Inoue, Hayashi, and Iwai families, participated in special performances as *jiutai* (chorus chanters). This marked the beginning of a new relationship that led them to seek apprenticeship with the Kanze-dayū. These new students traveled to Edo to train in the art directly at the Kanze-dayū's residence. After completing their training, they returned to Kyoto to teach amateurs, expanding the reach and influence of the Kanze school.[47] Motoakira exerted control over even his direct disciples, insisting on their strict adherence to a hierarchical system reinforced by step-by-step written commitments.

Motoakira's supervision and publication of the revised chant book was primarily aimed at disseminating the formal chants of the Edo Kanze school to local students. Although he was criticized for his efforts, the allure of studying under the Edo Kanze-*dayū* remained a significant draw for chant enthusiasts, ensuring that the desire of individuals to become apprentices did not wane.

Those who had no particular interest in learning nō chant or dance still had opportunities to enjoy nō. In the Edo

FIGURE 4 *An example of* machi-iri nō*: commoners (in the fenced area to the left of the stage) watch* Okina *at Edo Castle.* Chōnin onō haiken no zu. *Color woodblock print by Yōshū Chikanobu, 1889. Private collection.*

period, there were basically three ways for people outside the nobility to experience nō as spectators.[48] The first was through *machi-iri nō*, events in which official nō performances at *daimyō* castles were occasionally opened to townspeople (Figure 4). At these events, lunch boxes and umbrellas were often distributed to attendees. The second was *kanjin nō*, or subscription nō, in which, with the permission of the shogunate, a temporary stage was built in an empty plot of land where the townspeople lived and nō was performed for the general public.[49]

In Edo, tickets for nō performances that allowed the audience to sit on *tatami* (called *tatami fuda*) were compulsorily allocated to the townspeople. For example, in 1750 a *kanjin nō* performance organized by Kanze Motoakira in Edo lasted 15 days, and the number of *tatami fuda* allocated to each town was 300 per day for plank seats. In addition, 3,000 *irekomi fuda* (standing tickets) were allotted each day. Not only townspeople but also the shogun and samurai paid for their tickets. The number of visitors exceeded 5,000 per day, and up to 10,000 people came to see the popular play *Dōjōji*.

One document detailing other *kanjin nō* describes the audience in a frenzy because they could not understand what was being said, and "people who brought in bedclothes and fell asleep," "people who brought in sake and got drunk," and "people who snored deeply. When the shogun or famous samurai entered, the audience would look away from the stage and focus on them, shouting loudly."[50]

The third way townspeople could access nō was by watching performances by unofficial actors, often from the lower social classes. These performances were known as *tsuji nō* (crossroads nō). One of the most famous examples of this type of performance is that of Horii Sensuke (dates unknown), active in the early eighteenth century, who received official training in nō but borrowed elements from kabuki and puppet theatre in his nō performances. Some of the official actors petitioned the shogunate to ban the performance of Sensuke nō, arguing that it lowered the dignity of the art.[51] In certain areas, the appointment of a leader who was a patron of nō led to an increase in opportunities for nō performances in a city, and the culture of learning nō flourished among its residents. The lasting influence of these Edo-era clan lords can still be seen in areas such as Kyushu, Kanazawa, Shikoku, Okayama, Hiroshima, and Owari.

Nō theatre during the decline of the shogunate

During the late Edo period the shogunate faced financial difficulties. In March 1789 it issued a decree against further embellishment of nō costumes as part of a broader austerity measure that also applied to official nō actors. As a result, the frequency of nō performances at Edo Castle declined, creating challenges for the actors of the five troupes. To overcome these difficulties, the fifteenth head of the Hōshō school, Tomoyuki (1799–1863), organized *kanjin nō* performances outside the Sujikaibashi gate of Edo Castle in 1848 to support the actors and preserve the tradition in the midst of this difficult time.

This was the last *kanjin nō* of the Edo period.[52] A picture scroll illustrates the large gathering of townspeople at the spacious venue where it was staged.[53]

Despite attracting audiences, these *kanjin* nō performances yielded minimal profits due to the high costs associated with organizing them. Faced with these financial pressures, some official performers turned to teaching amateur apprentices as an alternative source of income. This was especially true for chorus singers, who traveled to rural villages to directly accept amateur students, thereby spreading their art, and ensuring its continuation even in difficult times.

Beginning on December 2, 1858, the fourteenth shogun, Iemochi (1846–1866), celebrated his proclamation with a nō performance. Five consecutive days of performances were scheduled over a period of three months. During this period, the regular New Year's chanting ceremony also took place, albeit in an abbreviated format. The context for this extended celebration was complex: the arrival of Commodore Matthew Perry in 1853, sent by the United States to force Japan to open its borders; the controversial signing of the unequal Treaty of Amity and Commerce between Japan and the United States on June 19, 1858; and intense opposition to Iemochi's leadership, especially from Hitotsubashi Yoshinobu (1837–1913), who would become the last shogun, and his faction. On March 21, 1862 a nō performance was organized at the Tōshōgū shrine in Nikkō, marking the last official performance of the Tokugawa government. In 1866, when Yoshinobu was proclaimed shogun, the traditional ceremonial nō was not held.

Modernization

Impact of the Meiji Restoration on nō

In the nineteenth century, as Western countries expanded into East Asia, the faction that supported the emperor and opposed the old Tokugawa regime insisted on the restoration of political power to the emperor. In 1867 the Tokugawa government, sensing the deteriorating situation, announced that it would return power to the emperor, a move that resulted in all nō artists employed by the shogunate being suddenly dismissed from their jobs. To survive, some were forced to sell their nō masks and costumes, which were essential to their performances; others changed profession; still others simply stopped performing. In the early years of the new Meiji government, traditional culture was often sidelined in the rush to modernize the state in accordance with Western standards. During this period, many nō masks and costumes ended up in the hands of international collectors and museums around the world, where they remain today.

On November 27, 1871 the Tokyo prefectural government, acting on behalf of the former Edo shogunate, officially notified the nō performers of their dismissal. This marked the end of a long era of steady economic and political sponsorship. However, an opportunity for reintegration into the system was offered: If they registered their status by September 25, they could be rehired by the new government as *chōshin*, or courtiers of the emperor. Recognizing the historical significance of nō and its past contributions, the imperial family extended its support and offered the performers protection during this time of transition. However, nō actors, who were deeply integrated into samurai society and committed to the warrior class, were reluctant to abandon their long-standing allegiance to the Tokugawa family and accept employment in the imperial household. Ultimately, only thirty-eight actors applied for *chōshin* status; among them were the prominent actors Kita Roppeita (1814–1869) and Umewaka Minoru (1828–1909).

In 1871 statesman Iwakura Tomomi (1825–1883) and his delegation embarked on what became known as the Iwakura Mission, a diplomatic trip to Europe and the United States aimed at revising unequal treaties and studying Western government, technology, and culture in order to modernize Japan. During their visit they were treated to opera performances, which made them realize the importance of performing arts as a cultural and diplomatic tool in the West. Inspired by this, Iwakura sought to reestablish nō as the representative performing art of Japan, to be presented to foreign dignitaries during their official visits to the country. With the support of the Empress Dowager Eishō (1835–1897), a lover of nō, they sought the patronage of the imperial family and the aristocracy. In 1878, as part of their efforts to promote nō, a stage was built at Aoyama Palace for performances for the emperor.

However, this attempt to position nō as a national institution was not successful. The Edo shogunate had patronized nō as ceremonial entertainment to maintain samurai order, but the new government abandoned the traditional system, establishing the country on legal and institutional principles inspired by Western countries. Some politicians, such as the first prime minister Itō Hirobumi (1841–1909), Foreign Minister Inoue Kaoru (1836–1915), and key business leaders such as Shibusawa Eiichi (1840–1931), favored showcasing kabuki rather than nō to foreign guests. The Meiji government wanted to create a "new" Japan, so modernizing kabuki became a priority rather than supporting nō. However, figures such as Iwakura Tomomi recognized the cultural importance of nō and made efforts to preserve its tradition. Furthermore, influential nobles who championed nō as a performing art worthy of international recognition successfully lobbied for its renaming as nōgaku (consisting of nō and kyōgen), replacing the outdated and potentially misleading label of *sarugaku,* and establishing a protective framework for nō by founding the Nōgakusha (Nōgaku Association) in 1881.

In the same year the establishment of the Shiba nō Theatre (Shiba nōgakudō) on the former Edo shogunate grounds in Momijiyama in 1881, overseen by shareholders, marked a decisive step in providing a public platform for nō performances. It was the first theatre hall to combine Japanese and Western architecture, and the first example of the modern "building-within-a-building" nō hall we know today. In 1896 the Nōgakusha evolved into the Nōgakukai, whose main purpose was to support professional performers.[54] Supported by former feudal lords, the aristocracy, and *zaibatsu* (industrial conglomerate) tycoons who had amassed wealth in the early period of industrialization, nō gradually experienced a resurgence. Financial support from amateur disciples in Kyoto, Osaka, and other provincial cities, operating within the *iemoto* system established during the Edo period, also helped alleviate the economic hardships faced by the performers of the four troupes.

As Japan underwent a process of increasing Westernization, a yearning for its traditional culture began to surface. Once considered antiquated, ancient Japanese cultural practices experienced a revival, fueled by a renewed sense of national pride following Japan's victories in the Sino-Japanese War (1894–1895) and the Russo-Japanese War (1904–1905). The first performances of nō outside Japan took place during this period in the occupied territories (*gaichi*).[55]

Since the discovery and publication of Zeami's treatises in 1908, there has been a marked tendency to emphasize the spirituality and emotional depth of nō plays, and the length of performances has tended to increase as actors have adopted a more detailed style. During the Taishō period (1912–1926), nō experienced a boom in popularity among the general public. In addition to professional performances, there were numerous amateur events such as "Gentlemen's nō," "Ladies' nō," and "Students' nō," which allowed enthusiasts from diverse backgrounds to engage in this traditional art form. Many skilled female nō enthusiasts were featured in magazines dedicated to the art. As long as these women were exceptional students and practiced nō as a form of learning, their activities were positively received. This contributed to the image of nō as an open and inclusive art form.

After the Meiji Restoration, Kiyotaka (1837–1888), the *iemoto* of the Kanze school, moved to Shizuoka in the same area where the Tokugawa family resided. As a result, Umewaka Minoru I (1828–1909) and Kanze Tetsunojō IV (1843–1911) assumed leadership in Tokyo and started issuing licenses in

Kiyotaka's place. This transition was seen as problematic. As a consequence, in 1920 Minoru, Tetsunojō, and their students founded the independent Umewaka school. However, the Nōgakukai forbade them to perform under the banner of the Umewaka school. Subsequently, with the support of nō patrons, there was a gradual movement toward dissolving the Umewaka school, and in 1932 all the actors associated with the Umewaka school rejoined the Kanze school. This series of events became famously known as the *kanbai* issue (*kan* stands for the Kanze school, *bai* is another reading of the character for *ume* in Umewaka) and sparked a debate on the merits and drawbacks of the *iemoto* system.

Meanwhile, the stylistic beauty and poetic-dramatic form of nō attracted attention in the West in the late nineteenth and early twentieth centuries, further increasing the general recognition of nō as an important art form. As foreign observers visited Japan and were exposed to nō, their fascination with it grew and spread abroad. The American art historian Ernest Fenollosa (1853–1908), who moved to Japan in the 1870s, played a key role in the Japanese art conservation movement and had a deep appreciation for nō. His early translations of nō plays were later edited and published by American poet Ezra Pound (1885–1972), with an introduction by Irish poet and playwright William Butler Yeats (1865–1939).[56] In 1916 Yeats produced *At the Hawk's Well*, which fused Celtic lore with nō aesthetics. After him, other modernists sought inspiration from nō to create works that would distance them from Western naturalism. Among such works were *The Woman and Her Shadow* (*La femme et son ombre*, first version 1922) by Paul Claudel (1868–1955) and *He Who Said Yes* (*Der Jasager*, 1929) by Bertolt Brecht (1898–1956) and Kurt Weill (1900–1950). In France, Jacques Copeau (1879–1949) and his company were attracted to the use of the body and mask in nō, an interest that was passed on to later artists, including Jacques Lecoq (1921–1999) and, in turn, Ariane Mnouchkine.[57]

In the first half of the twentieth century, nō was hailed as a symbol of the "Japanese spirit," a sentiment that intensified with the rising tide of nationalism and militarization in the 1930s and 1940s. During this period, all forms of theatre, including nō, were used for war propaganda and subjected to strict censorship. In 1941 a political initiative to honor war casualties led to the commissioning of nō plays such as *Chūrei* (*Loyal Spirits*) to commemorate the fallen through the construction of memorial towers nationwide. In 1943 the scope of this commissioning expanded with *Miikusa-bune* (*Imperial Warship*), a play sponsored by the Imperial Japanese Navy Information Department and staged throughout Japan to bolster support for the war effort.[58] Conversely, nō works that featured the emperor and the imperial family, such as *Semimaru* and *Ohara gokō*, came under scrutiny for depictions that were deemed inappropriate. Recent studies have shown a continued appreciation for nō singing in the occupied territories of Manchukuo, Taiwan, and Korea, among Japanese communities in Brazil, and even in internment camps in the United States.[59]

Nō after the Second World War

In the 600 years since the time of Kan'ami and Zeami, nō has gradually evolved in response to changes in politics, the environment, tradition, and its audience. Until the Meiji and Taishō periods, it was widely believed that nō should remain distinct from other performing arts. However, there was a shift in opinion that advocated wider accessibility beyond the cultural elite. This led to the idea that performing nō in a variety of settings could introduce the art form to a wider audience.

The Nohgaku Performers' Association (Nōgaku Kyōkai) was founded in September 1945 with the aim of preserving the traditions of nō and kyōgen, facilitating their transmission, and promoting cooperation among its members. Initially, the professional field of nō was exclusively male, but in 1948 several female performers were allowed to join the association, among whom was Tsumura Kimiko (1902–1974).[60]

Another significant milestone occurred in 1950 with the enactment of the Law for the Protection of Cultural Properties. This initiative, the first of its kind in Japan, recognized intangible cultural heritage and officially recognized nō as protected cultural property.

The first nō performance in the West took place at the Venice International Theatre Festival in August 1954, marking the beginning of a new era of intercultural exchange. Since then, performances and workshops have taken place in many countries. In 1957 nōgaku was declared an Important Intangible Cultural Property by the Japanese government, leading to the establishment of the Nihon Nōgakukai (Japan Nōgaku Association), whose membership is reserved for experienced performers.

After the Second World War, the novelist Mishima Yukio (1925–1970) contributed significantly to the fusion of traditional and contemporary art forms by writing "modern nō plays" (*Kindai nōgakushū*, 1956). This effort was paralleled by the involvement of esteemed nō and kyōgen actors in artforms and media other than nō. For example, in 1962 Kanze Hisao (1925–1978) spent a period of study in France, where he became acquainted with Jean Louis Barrault.[61] Hisao and kyōgen actor Nomura Mansaku also appeared in Takechi Tetsuji's performance of Arnold Schönberg's *Pierrot Lunaire* (*Tsuki ni tsukareta Piero*, 1955). Among others, Hisao's brother Hideo (1927–2007) and, more recently, Nomura Mansai have also been involved in the production of films and TV series. Their participation has highlighted nō's unique aesthetics, vocal techniques, and physical movements, bringing wider recognition to the art form's distinctive qualities.

Western theatre practitioners continued to be inspired by the rich traditions of nō. There are numerous examples, and we will highlight a few notable cases. British composer Benjamin Britten (1913–1976) was one of the numerous Western composers to be inspired by nō. During his visit to Japan in 1955 he attended performances of the nō play *Sumidagawa*, which led to the creation of the "church parable" *Curlew River* (1964), with a libretto by William Plomer. *Curlew River* has been performed by various companies, often together with a production of *Sumidagawa*. Peter Brook (1925–2022), influenced by nō's minimalism, has worked particularly with Japanese actor Yoshi Oida, incorporating elements of nō into his productions. Robert Wilson incorporated aspects of nō into his avant-garde opera *CIVIL warS* (1984), reflecting its aesthetic influence. Eugenio Barba, through his work in intercultural theatre, has engaged with nō, organizing performances with nō actors, including Kanze Hideo, and blending theatrical traditions. Ariane Mnouchkine, with her Théâtre du Soleil, has embraced nō in her play *L'île d'or*, demonstrating its strong influence. Recently, there has been a renewed interest in nō among contemporary artists, including Japanese directors who have created new plays strongly influenced by nō. For example, Noda Hideki's *The Diver* (2007), a modern adaptation of the play *Ama*, also borrows from nō staging techniques, while Okada Toshiki's *Nō Theater* (2018) was created using nō dramaturgical principles.

Despite its lasting impact on Japan's theatre landscape, the cultural elements nō contains, such as classical literature, religious insights, and traditional practices, have become increasingly distant to modern audiences. This situation, coupled with the declining prestige of nō as a marker of cultural status among the middle class, has led to a decline in audience numbers and poses a challenge to the economic livelihood of performers. The designation of nō as part of UNESCO's Intangible Cultural Heritage in 2008 underscored its importance as a cultural treasure, albeit one that may be perceived as belonging to a bygone era.

In 2012 efforts to rejuvenate traditional culture led to a revision of the Basic Education Law, which promotes the integration of traditional culture into the curriculum of elementary, middle, and high schools. Despite this initiative, a major challenge remains. There is a shortage of educators skilled in teaching nō chant and music. Western music has dominated the teaching curricula since the Meiji period, making it difficult to incorporate Japanese traditional music into modern education. To address this issue, the Nohgaku

Performers' Association is proactively sending actors to schools to conduct workshops for both students and teachers.

The National Noh Theatre (Kokuritsu Nōgakudō) was established in Tokyo in 1983 with the aim of preserving, disseminating, and promoting the practice of nōgaku. It is not only a performance venue but also a center for research, education, and training. Since 1984 it has hosted a training program for *waki*, musicians, and kyōgen actors. The theatre hosts a variety of events, including regular performances, workshops, and exhibitions, designed to deepen the appreciation of nō among audiences of all ages.

When professional female nō performers began to be recognized, controversy arose over whether women should wear makeup on stage. Some argued that women could not express the powerful physicality and low voices characteristic of male performers. Even when allowed to sit in the chorus, women sometimes refrained from singing due to concerns about differences in vocal quality. However, more and more female professional nō performers, such as Kanze school actors Uzawa Hisa and her daughter Hikaru, have strived through practice and hard work to achieve the same strength and low register as their male counterparts. It was not until 2005 that female nō performers were finally allowed to join the Japan Nōgaku Association.[62]

Moreover, the proliferation of social networks and video streaming platforms, as well as the many forms of collaboration between nō and the world of anime and manga, allow artists to connect with audiences that were previously unreachable. Examples include the *VR Noh Kōkaku Kidōtai* (2020), based on Masamune Shirow's popular manga and anime series *Ghost in the Shell*, and the animation film *Inuō* (2021, directed by Yuasa Masaaki), based on the Muromachi period actor Inuō. Despite facing challenges, nō retains a deep appeal and a history of flexible adaptation to changing social contexts. With its deep cultural significance and the enduring fascination with it, nō has the potential to remain relevant and adaptable in future eras, continuing its legacy within and beyond Japan's borders.

2

Plays

An essential resource for the study of nō is play chant books (*utaibon*), many of which became widely available during the Edo period thanks to the development of the print industry, and choreography books (*tsuke*), traditionally passed down within the families of actors. Plays in the current repertory (*genkō kyoku*) are published as *utaibon*, with the official authorization of the *iemoto*, the head of a school. These publications are available for purchase and are widely used by amateur practitioners. There are also various annotated anthologies of nō plays featuring running commentary and contemporary Japanese versions. Additionally, translations are available in several non-Japanese languages.[1]

Despite the abundance of resources, tracing the origins of nō playwriting is a difficult task because of the scarcity of written documents on nō before Zeami's time. Although we know from historical sources that *sarugaku* was performed before the time of Kan'ami and Zeami, the absence of written scripts before Zeami suggests that *sarugaku* performers, who formed traveling companies that served temples and shrines, had low literacy and that the plays were probably transmitted only orally.

However, from Zeami's writings it can be deduced that certain plays in the current repertory predate his era. For example, in the treatise *Go on* (*Five Sorts of Singing*), he notes that the nō *Ominameshi* was originally written by a performer known as Kia (dates unknown, also known as Kiami).[2] In *Sarugaku Dangi* (*Talks on Sarugaku*), Zeami attributes the authorship of a play called *Shii no shōshō*, which would later be known as *Kayoi Komachi*, to an unnamed monk, adding that Kan'ami rewrote it. In the same passage he also states that the plays *Ukai* and *Kashiwazaki* were initially composed by Saemon Gorō of the Enami troupe, but also that, since Zeami "cut out the bad passages and inserted better ones, they should be considered as his works."[3] Zeami's writings contain numerous other mentions of earlier authors, suggesting that several plays in the repertory during his time were subsequently rewritten or modified, perhaps even several times. This makes it difficult to attribute authorship to a single playwright. As a consequence, about half of the current repertory is considered to be of unknown or uncertain authorship. What is clear, however, is that most *sarugaku* actors were also playwrights, composers of music, and choreographers of the plays they performed.[4]

Repertory and categorization

The current nō repertory, which varies slightly between schools, consists of approximately 240 plays, with the majority originating from the Muromachi period.[5] These are only a few of the several hundred that have been written since the fourteenth century, when plays began to be recorded on paper.[6] Of these, about 120 plays are performed regularly today and are therefore more familiar to audiences. The current repertory was selected through a process of refinement that lasted for centuries, during which plays fell in and out of favor. Plays that are considered "standard" today may have been less popular or rarely performed in earlier periods. While performance techniques such as choreography or chant have evolved over time, the text of the plays has remained largely the same.

Most nō plays share a similar plot structure, and characters are typically built around defined role-types, such as the male deity, the female celestial being, the fallen warrior, the madwoman, or the dragon deity. Some of these role-types already existed in Zeami's time, as he discusses them in *Nikyoku santai ningyōzu* (*Figure Drawings of the Two Arts and the Three Modes*; see Chapter 1, Kan'ami and Zeami, and Figure 3). These roles are performed with specific mask and costume combinations, making them easily recognizable to the knowledgeable audience. Formalization sets expectations for how a play will unfold. Recurring plots serve as a framework for telling stories about specific characters, often drawn from historical or fictional narratives that were already well known at the time the plays were composed. While certain common features and underlying structures can be identified, exceptions are frequent, making it difficult to formulate universal guidelines for interpreting plays. Each play is unique, often distinguished by memorable lines, specific features in the *shite*'s mask and costume, or distinctive stage properties.

Nō plays are traditionally grouped into categories according to structural or thematical similarities. In the following sections we introduce two main types of repertory categorization: the *gobandate* system, based on the type of *shite*, and the *mugen-genzai* grouping, based on the play structure. It is useful to keep in mind that the categorization of nō plays is a retrospective analytical tool rather than a set of prescriptive guidelines, as these categories were established after most plays were already written and performed.

The *gobandate* system

It is common for a combination of several nō and kyōgen plays to be performed on the same day, a tradition that dates back to the origins of nō and continues to the present. The categorization of the nō repertory known as the *gobandate* or "five-play system," established in the Edo period but with its roots in Zeami's time, determines the performance order. Zeami believed that plays featuring deities should be performed at the beginning because of their auspicious quality, and that the structure of a program should progress from slower and more formal plays at the beginning to faster and more dynamic plays at the end.[7] According to the *gobandate* system, the repertory is divided into five categories based on the nature of the *shite* and the general atmosphere of the play. The ritual performance of *Okina* is regarded as a special piece, outside these five categories.[8] The progression follows the *jo-ha-kyū* rhythm, a principle derived from *gagaku* court music that governs the pacing of a performance or event, which was also mentioned by Zeami.[9] *Jo* (beginning) is a slow opening, *ha* (break) is an elaborate development, and *kyū* (fast) is a swift conclusion.

Table 1 lists the five categories of nō plays, which are commonly referred to sequentially as first category (*shobanme mono*), second category (*nibanme mono*), and so on. In

TABLE 1 *The* gobandate *play categorization.*

Category			Examples
First	*Shobanme mono, waki nō, kami nō*	Deities	*Awaji, Ema, Kamo, Takasago, Tsurukame, Yōrō*
Second	*Nibanme mono, shura nō*	Ghosts of warriors	*Atsumori, Ebira, Tamura, Tomoe, Tsunemasa, Yashima*
Third	*Sanbanme mono, kazura nō*	Female spirits	*Hashitomi, Hagoromo, Izutsu, Nonomiya, Sotoba Komachi, Yuya*
Fourth	*Yonbanme mono, zatsu nō*	Miscellaneous	*Aoinoue, Ataka, Jinen koji, Miidera, Mochizuki, Sumidagawa*
Fifth	*Gobanme mono, kiri nō*	Ending	*Adachigahara (Kurozuka), Kurama Tengu, Shakkyō, Tōru, Tsuchigumo, Yamanba*

Japanese, each category may have an alternative name based on its distinctive characteristics, such as *shura nō* ("plays about warriors in hell") for the second category, or *kazura nō* ("wig plays") for the third category.[10] The following section introduces the plot structure and main features of each category.[11]

First category (deities)

Since Zeami's time, nō performance events used to begin with *Okina*, followed by a deity play.[12] These also came to be called *waki nō* (lit. "side nō") because they were performed directly after *Okina*.[13] This tradition is still observed today for particularly formal occasions. These plays feature a deity as the *shite* and are characterized by a solemn and celebratory atmosphere. The story opens with the *waki*, usually a Shintō priest or an imperial envoy, visiting a renowned location. There he encounters a local person, often an elderly man (*mae shite—shite* in the first act) who tells him the history of the place. This is actually the local deity in disguise, revealing their true identity in the second act (*nochi shite—shite* in the second act), and performing a dance (e.g., *kami mai*, *gaku*) in celebration. The play ends with auspicious words that bless the land and the emperor's reign. The performance of these plays is often characterized by the use of stage properties that illustrate the setting, such as a mountain or a building. The second act features the *taiko* stick drum, emphasizing the miraculous appearance of the deity.

Zeami's *Takasago* exemplifies the themes and structure characteristic of this category of plays. In the first act, a Shintō priest and his companions (*waki* and *waki tsure*) visit Takasago, a seaside location located in today's Hyōgo prefecture, and encounter an elderly couple (*mae shite* and *tsure*) tending a sacred pine tree. After exchanging poems, the couple reveal themselves to be the spirits of the famous pines of Takasago and Sumiyoshi, and then disappear. A local man (*ai kyōgen*) then tells the story of the paired pines (*aioi no matsu*). In the second act the priest and his companions reach

Sumiyoshi, where the deity of the Sumiyoshi Shrine (*nochi shite*) appears and performs a dance to bless the emperor's reign. The Sumiyoshi deity was revered as the patron of sailing and Japanese poetry, a theme reflected in the play. Zeami interwove in the lyrics quotes from the preface to the imperial poem anthology *Kokin wakashū*, which mentions the paired pines and describes how every living being is capable of composing verse, and how poetry "stirs the emotions of the invisible spirits and gods, brings harmony to relations between men and women, and calms the hearts of fierce warriors."[14]

Central to this play is the celebration of peaceful governance, epitomized by a prosperous land and the achievement of harmony among all beings.[15] Although nō plays do not contain explicit dedications, playwrights sought to praise specific shoguns who supported their art.[16] This political content is conveyed through the metaphor of marital relationships and longevity, symbolized by the pine trees of Takasago and Sumiyoshi in the Osaka-Hyōgo region. While the original message of the play may be less understandable to contemporary audiences, the more universal theme of harmonious marriage has gained prominence. In fact, some chant excerpts from *Takasago* are often performed during auspicious events, including wedding ceremonies.

Second category (ghosts of warriors)

In plays of the second category, the main characters are usually the ghosts of warriors who have fallen into the Buddhist hell of *shura*, where those who have sinned by taking life are condemned to relive their deeds.[17] Their end came in various ways: Some perished in battle, some were executed, while others chose suicide to avoid capture. These plays do not glorify military prowess or celebrate victories; instead, they delve into the deep anguish of those who lost their lives on the battlefield.[18] A prime example is *Atsumori*, analyzed later this volume. Plays of this type are minimal in their staging conventions: The *shite* often appears alone (without *tsure*), the orchestra usually does not include the *taiko*, and stage properties are rarely used.

These stories draw inspiration from medieval warrior chronicles, particularly *The Tale of the Heike*, which details the historic conflict between the rival Minamoto and Taira clans. Nō playwrights often interpreted or freely expanded these tales. Typically, the *waki* is a traveling monk who visits a location associated with the *shite*, where he encounters a local person who is later revealed to be the ghost of a warrior. In the second half of the play, the ghost reappears in their real form (*nochi shite*) and reenacts the battle in which they perished or recounts another significant event from their life. This section often includes a dance in which the *shite* circles the stage (*kakeri*) to express their anguish.

Zeami wrote several plays of this kind.[19] His approach shifted the portrayal of warriors from demonic figures to more nuanced and psychologically complex human characters. This evolution was in keeping with the aesthetic tastes of the warrior elite who were emerging as the new patrons of nō. Notably, only one play in the second category, *Tomoe*, features a female protagonist, the famous warrior Tomoe Gozen. In addition, other military tales that depict characters as living within the narrative, and not as ghosts, are presented as *genzai nō* and fall into the fourth category of plays.

Third category (female spirits)

At the center of the *gobandate* system, the third category is considered the most elegant and refined. The protagonist here is a female character, such as the ghost of a woman or the spirit of a plant.[20] These plays are also called *kazura mono*, named after the *kazura* (wig) tied in a knot at the back of the neck that is recurring feature of these roles. Similar to the second category, the staging is simple, although these plays sometimes feature a stage property. The performance is characterized by a slow pace and minimal movement, emphasizing chant and abstract dance over action, making these nō particularly challenging for actors, as well as for the audience. In the second act the *shite* performs a slow dance to instrumental music, such as *jo no mai* or *chū no mai*. While most of these plays follow the two-part structure of *mugen nō*, a few, such as *Yuya*, are *genzai nō*. Among their sources are poetry anthologies, as well as the Heian period novel *The Tale of Genji*, which offers material for fourteen nō in the current repertory.[21]

The *shite* appearing in plays in the third category are often portrayed as being trapped by unresolved emotions, grappling with intense attachment to their past. Similar to the way warriors are haunted by traumatic events that occurred in their earthly lives, female characters seek salvation and release from their emotional bonds. From a Buddhist perspective, this attachment is seen negatively, as it hinders liberation from the cycle of reincarnation. In this context, the *waki*, often a monk, helps the *shite* in reaching enlightenment.

One of the most famous plays of the third category is *Izutsu*, which is based on the poetry collection *Tales of Ise* (ninth–tenth century). On a moonlit night, a traveling monk (*waki*) visits the Ariwara Temple in Nara, where he prays for the repose of the court poet Ariwara no Narihira and his wife, who once lived in the area. A woman (*mae shite*) appears and offers flowers and holy water to the grave of Narihira, represented by an old well, as she recounts various episodes in the *Tales of Ise*. There was a time when Narihira went to visit a lover in a distant province, but his wife composed a poem dissuading him from continuing his travels. Even earlier, when the two were children, they played around a well until they promised to become husband and wife. The woman turns out to be the ghost of Narihira's wife, then disappears into the well. As the monk falls asleep, the ghost of Narihira's wife (*nochi shite*) reappears, dressed in the cloak and hat Narihira left her as a keepsake. Overcome by nostalgia, she dances, reminiscing the past. As her memories surface, she approaches the well and looks down, seeing herself dressed as her husband, before disappearing with the first light of dawn.

Although numerous female characters in nō are portrayed as young and beautiful, there are significant exceptions, particularly the plays in which the poetess Ono no Komachi (825–900) is depicted in her later years as an old woman yet retaining her wit and knowledge (*Sekidera Komachi*, *Sotoba Komachi*, and *Ōmu Komachi*). Plays featuring old characters have a high *kurai* and are known for their complexity and depth; hence only highly accomplished and mature actors perform them.

Fourth category (miscellaneous)

The fourth category is also called miscellaneous (*zatsu*) because it includes numerous different themes and types of *shite*.[22] The arbitrariness of this category suggests that when the *gobandate* system was created, it was not so much a matter of grouping plays together as of establishing an order of performance. This category contains almost all of the *genzai nō* pieces in the repertory. Among the subgroups that can be identified are the madness (*kyōran* or *monogurui*) pieces, in which the *shite* has become deranged for various reasons, including separation from a lover or child. With the exception of *Sumidagawa*, madness plays end with a reunion of the characters. Another subcategory features warriors who, unlike in second-category plays, are alive in the present time. These plays tend to extol military virtues such as the loyalty between lord and vassal.

In *Ataka*, Minamoto no Yoshitsune, who has achieved great victories against the Taira clan, is pursued by the army of his brother Yoritomo. Yoshitsune (portrayed by a *kokata* child actor) and his loyal follower Benkei (*shite*, unmasked), along with other retainers, disguise themselves as mountain priests and seek refuge in northern Japan. Learning of their escape, Yoritomo orders checkpoints to be set up to catch them. When the party tries to cross the Ataka barrier, guarded by Togashi (*waki*), Benkei cleverly claims they are traveling to collect donations. Despite Togashi's suspicions, Benkei's bold reading of a makeshift subscription list (*kanjinchō*) and his forceful rebuke of Yoshitsune, who is disguised as a porter, convince Togashi to let them pass. After crossing the checkpoint, Togashi sends them *sake* as an apology for detaining them, and the group has a banquet at which Benkei dances. Remaining cautious, Benkei leads the group to continue their escape. This play praises Benkei's wit and loyalty to Yoshitsune, while subtly suggesting that Togashi may have recognized the party. Moved by Yoshitsune's plight and Benkei's unwavering loyalty, Togashi may have sympathized with them and allowed them to pass.

The fourth category also includes plays in which the *shite* is a supernatural being, although the structure does not always follow that of *mugen* plays. This group includes pieces in which a resentful spirit appears to reenact its grudge or plays in which the *shite* is a female deity performing the *kagura* dance. In *Aoinoue*, an early play that Zeami later revised, Lady Aoi, the wife of Prince Genji and who is haunted by an evil spirit, falls gravely ill. Efforts to cure her through prayers and rituals prove fruitless. Teruhi (*tsure*), a shaman, is summoned to identify the source of her illness. As she begins her incantation, the living spirit of Rokujō no Miyasudokoro (*mae shite*), Genji's former lover, appears, consumed by jealousy and resentment. As Aoi's condition worsens, a priest from Mt. Hiei (*waki*) is summoned. He confronts Lady Rokujō's spirit, now transformed into a vengeful demon (*nochi shite*, wearing the *Hannya* mask), and subdues it after a fierce battle. Lady Rokujō is able to rid herself of her attachments and prepare for enlightenment.[23]

Fifth category (ending)

This category is also called *kiri nō* (ending nō) because its plays are the last in the program.[24] These plays are often shorter, contain more action scenes, and typically feature supernatural characters such as demons, *tengu* (mythical creatures endowed with supernatural powers), or dragon deities. These features follow the *jo-ha-kyū* progression, with the *kyū* phase providing a high-paced sharp conclusion to the cycle. Some plays in this category, such as *Adachigahara* (also known as *Kurozuka*) or *Tsuchigumo*, feature monsters that are ultimately defeated by the *waki*. Although the atmosphere of fifth-category plays may not be as celebratory as those in the first category, since they serve as the conclusion of a performance event, they usually have a "happy ending." The categorization of nō plays, especially in the fourth and fifth categories, may vary according to the stylistic interpretations of different schools. Nevertheless, they complete a thematic cycle that begins with deity-centered narratives. This characteristic is so pronounced that certain fifth-category plays, especially those involving dragon deities, have a similar atmosphere as first-category plays. The end of one cycle suggests the beginning of another.

An example of ending nō is *Shakkyō* (*The Stone Bridge*). The priest Jakushō (*waki*) travels to the foot of Mt. Shōryō in China, where he reaches a narrow stone bridge that crosses a deep gorge. The bridge is said to lead to the paradise of Monju, the Bodhisattva of Wisdom. An old woodcutter (*mae shite*) appears and tells the story of the mystical bridge, explaining that only holy men should cross it, alluding to the rigors of Buddhist ascetic practice. He urges Jakushō to wait, for he will witness a miraculous event. Shortly thereafter mythical lions (*nochi shite* and *tsure*), messengers of the Bodhisattva Monju, appear and dance, frolicking among the peonies that grow around the bridge. Plays such as *Shakkyō* are often presented as half nō (*han nō*), with only the second act staged, which suits their placement in the *jo-ha-kyū* pattern.

Mugen nō and *genzai nō*

In the early twentieth century, a new categorization based on the concept of *mugen* ("dream and illusion") emerged. This term was introduced to define a type of play in which the *shite* is a supernatural character who appears in disguise in the first act, disappears in the middle of it, and reappears in true form in the second act. This type of play is contrasted with that of *genzai* (present time) plays, in which all the characters are living human beings. Scholars emphasized the concept of *mugen* as a key element distinguishing nō from other traditional Japanese theatrical forms, such as kabuki. This emphasis gained importance during a period of heightened nationalism, and also served as a counterpoint to Western theatre. As described in Chapter 1, the *mugen* format was perfected by Zeami, thus consolidating his general recognition as the "father of nō."[25]

Mugen nō

In *mugen* plays, the *shite* is connected to a temporal realm different from the present setting in which the *waki* resides. The *shite* may be a ghost (an entity bridging past and present), a deity, or some other kind of abstract being such as the spirit of a plant (existing in a timeless dimension) that evokes and reenacts past events before the *waki*. Rather than unfolding as a flashback or time-slip, this occurs through the storytelling of the *shite*, much like a "narrative within a narrative."

The reenactment of the past by the *shite* is often imbued with a sense of nostalgia for a joyful time that will not return, or with resentment for a painful event that has marked their lives. This points to a metanarrative quality of *mugen* in which characters are portrayed in the act of reflecting and responding to a story about themselves, struggling to process trauma. This is made even more intriguing by the fact that the *shite* is both the protagonist and the narrator of their own story. Thus, the concept of *mugen* seems to emphasize the "reflexive" nature of performance as a means of representing significant events that shape human life. In some cases the encounter between *shite* and *waki* leads to relief from such distress, represented by the *shite* achieving Buddhist enlightenment (as in, for example, *Atsumori*, *Kiyotsune*, or *Kakitsubata*). The healing process here is twofold, as it involves a psychological aspect, embodied in the act of storytelling, and a religious dimension, represented by the prayers offered by the monk. In other instances, however, a definitive resolution is lacking, and the play concludes with the *shite* simply disappearing at the conclusion of its presentation (e.g., *Yashima*, *Izutsu*, *Nonomiya*). In some cases, such plays conclude with lines suggesting that the events may actually be a dream experienced by the *waki*.

Dreams are a means by which spirits communicate with humans; therefore, in nō, they should not necessarily be interpreted as the *waki* actually falling asleep, but rather as a symbolic threshold where reality and fiction merge, and past and present intertwine. The dream motif also serves as a metaphor for the Buddhist concept of existential impermanence (*mujō*), including the ever-changing nature of existence and rebirth. The form of Buddhism adopted in Japan has evolved significantly over time. Initially focused on the protection of the state, it transitioned to emphasizing the salvation of sentient beings, then integrated with Shintō and other existing religious traditions, and finally evolved into Pure Land Buddhism, devoted to Buddha Amida. During the Kamakura and Muromachi periods, these Buddhist teachings deeply influenced Japanese conceptions of life and death. Life is understood as a continuum of past, present, and future, with the concept of karma (cause and effect, or action and retribution) linking these three temporal states. Actions in past lives shape present circumstances, while present behaviors determine future conditions. Take for example this passage from the latter half of *Atsumori*, where the young warrior appears before Renshō (Naozane).

> ATSUMORI […] I have come so far to be with you in order to clear karma that is real.
> RENSHŌ […] As for me,
> I have always called the Name for you.
> How could sinful karma afflict you still?[26]

Despite Renshō's devoted prayers in Amida's name, Atsumori is still affected by the negative karma that binds the two, fueled by resentment toward his murderer; he begs him to continue praying so that he may be freed from his attachment to his former life and its tragic ending.

Genzai nō

Though the aesthetics and narratives of *mugen* have become somewhat synonymous with the nō genre, the nō repertory also includes numerous plays that follow different dramaturgical conventions. *Genzai* (present time) plays, which feature exclusively living human characters acting in the narrative present, focus on relationships such as those between parent and child, husband and wife, or lord and retainer.

In *genzai* plays the action does not revolve solely around the *shite* but often involves multiple characters. The *waki* is not just a listener but actively interacts with the *shite* throughout the entire play. Numerous *genzai* plays emphasize dialogue, highlighting the interpersonal relationships within the plot. This is the case in *Sumidagawa*, where the action is propelled by the conversation between the mother, the ferryman, and the traveler.

Due to these features, *genzai nō* are often described as being more "theatrical," in contrast to the ritualistic formalization of *mugen* plays. However, it would be incorrect to assume that their development occurred chronologically after *mugen nō*. Famous *genzai* plays like *Sotoba Komachi*, *Hyakuman*, and *Jinen koji* were performed even before Zeami's time and are among the earliest in the current repertory.[27]

Genzai plays are infused with Buddhist and Confucianist thought. The bond between parent and child, for example, is seen as only occurring in the present life, leading to deep distress when parents are separated from their children: Without reunion in this life there is no chance of meeting in the next. Romantic relationships are seen as spanning more than one lifetime, with karma from past lives affecting connections and separations in the present life, leading individuals to blame past actions for unfulfilled desires or to place their hopes in future outcomes. Similarly, the bonds between lord and vassal, or master and disciple, are also considered to extend over multiple lifetimes, with loyalty and attachment having such a significant impact as to determine the fate of those involved.

Other categorizations

Nō scholar Yokomichi Mario identified a third category of play that combines elements from *mugen* and *genzai nō*, which he called *ryōgakari nō* (double function nō).[28] For instance, in the first half of the long-time favorite play *Funa Benkei* the *shite* is the dancer Shizuka Gozen, while in the second half it is the ghost of General Taira no Tomomori. Yokomichi also conceives of a play type he calls *reigen* (phantasmal experience), in which the *waki* not only witnesses the miraculous apparition of a supernatural character but also interacts directly with them, as in, for example, *Kokaji* and *Chikubushima*. Plays can be categorized by their seasonal setting, which evokes the emotions and cultural meanings of that season. They can also be grouped by central themes such as love, madness, or revenge.

Non-canonical plays

The numerous plays that did not become part of the current repertory are often referred to as *bangaikyoku* (non-canonical plays) or *haikyoku* (discarded plays). The distinction between "current" and "non-current" refers to performance practice. If a play is not staged for several years, experiential knowledge of its performance will be lost. Conversely, plays not performed for generations can be revived (*fukkyoku*) using their texts and choreography books, leveraging the shared performance conventions of nō. This allows for the reconstruction of "lost" plays by comparing them with similar existing ones.

Non-canonical plays remain of interest to historians and include those celebrating figures like the feudal lord and unifier of Japan Toyotomi Hideyoshi (e.g., *Akechi uchi* and *Hōjō*), commissioned by Hideyoshi himself. During the Edo period, feudal lords had plays written more for chanting than full-stage performances, often drawing on local legends to strengthen ties with their domains. Recent initiatives have successfully reintegrated many such historical works into the contemporary repertory. Plays written since the Meiji period, known as *shinsaku nō* (newly written *nō*), often draw on recent historical events, popular culture, or non-Japanese sources, and may result from collaborations between actors and authors who are not nō specialists. An example is the nō *Osero*, based on Shakespeare's *Othello*, adapted by Japanese classical literature scholar Izumi Noriko in 2016 (Figure 5) and featuring Tatsumi Manjirō. In the play, the ghosts of Othello

FIGURE 5 *Hōshō school actors Tatsumi Manjirō as Othello (right) and Waku Sōtarō as Desdemona (left) in Izumi Noriko's* shinsaku nō Osero *(Othello). Ōe nōgakudō, Kyoto. December 3, 2016. Photograph: courtesy of Fujiwara Chisa.*

and Desdemona appear. She offers forgiveness to him, but burdened by deep self-reproach, Othello is unable to accept her pardon, leading to even greater suffering.

Structures and themes

Act and scene subdivision

Today it is common to divide plays into three orders: *ba* (acts), *dan* (scenes), and *shōdan* (segments). A common narrative structure, especially in *mugen* plays, features two acts, though some plays consist of a single act.[29] In the first act (*mae ba*), the main character (*shite*) may appear in disguise (*mae shite*). This first act ends when the *mae shite* leaves the stage (*naka iri*). After this, a kyōgen actor usually takes center stage to perform an interlude called *ai* (literally, "in between"). The *nochi ba* (second act) usually begins with a "waiting song" (*machi utai*) sung by the *waki*. Then the *shite* returns with a different mask-costume combination, revealing its true or final form (*nochi shite*). Other plays consist of a single act, but there is often a subtle division between its first and second halves. Each act can be further divided into scenes (*dan*). It possible for a two-*ba* structure to identify five *dan* in each act, although this number can vary. *Dan* are defined by the actions performed by the *shite* and the *waki* and can in turn be divided into segments called *shōdan*, which are described in detail in Chapter 3, since they are related not only to the plot but also to the staging of the text.

Dan are structured according to the *jo-ha-kyū* principle, which guides the overall structure of the play as well as its smaller subdivisions, taking it from a slow beginning to a fast ending. *Jo-ha-kyū* refers to the "rhythm" of a play in a broader sense, encompassing both dramaturgy and performance. For example, a play begins with an empty space that is gradually filled with performers. The story unfolds through interactions between the characters, leading to a climax. At the end of the play the performers gradually leave the stage, returning it to its original state: an empty space. This completes the cycle of *jo-ha-kyū* and prepares the stage for a new beginning.

This dramaturgical structure already existed at the time of Zeami, who discusses it in his treatise *Sandō* (*The Three Courses*, 1423). By the end of the sixteenth century, the style of playwriting was formalized, allowing later authors to build on this system to create new plays. Zeami emphasizes compact and coherent thematic unity as a primary requirement for composing plays. He considers three elements: the seed (*tane*), the structure (*saku*, lit. "making"), and the writing (*sho*). The first step in writing is to choose the *shite*, who will be the center of dance and chant. For male roles, Zeami recommends to "consider Narihira, Kuronushi, Genji, and spirited nobles like them, and for the Women's Mode, Lady Ise, Komachi, Giō, Gijo, Shizuka, Hyakuman, and graceful ladies of their kind."[30] The characters mentioned here were renowned for proficiency in poetry or dance. About the "seed," Zeami notes: "a new play, what I would call a 'play script from scratch,' is written without any original source with its visual display, relying on such connections as can be made with famous places and legendary sites."[31]

Zeami postulates that, after the source is established, the author should decide on the structure of the play, based on a sequence of five scenes (*dan*), following the principle of *jo-ha-kyū*. These should consist of the following: an introduction (*jo*), including the *waki*'s self-introduction and travel song; three scenes of development (*ha*) when the *shite* (and possible companions) appear and are expressing feelings or circumstances; dialogue between the *waki* and *shite*, following which they sing in unison; a musical passage or narrative dance (*kusemai*); and a finale (*kyū*), featuring dynamic dancing or a fight sequence. In the twentieth century, scholars such as Yokomichi Mario and Omote Akira elaborated on Zeami's theory, identifying a recurrent five-*dan* structure in both the first and second acts. Table 2 displays different ways of interpreting

TABLE 2 *Act/scene model subdivision of a two-act* mugen *nō play.*

Act (*ba*)	**Scene (*dan*)**	***Jo-ha-kyū* Model 1**	***Jo-ha-kyū* Model 2**	**Content**
First (*mae ba*)	1	*Jo*	*Jo*	*Waki* enters and gives background information to the play
	2	*Ha* 1	*Ha* 1	*Shite* in disguise enters, gives a monologue
	3	*Ha* 2	*Ha* 2	*Waki* and *shite* interact in a dialogue
	4	*Ha* 2	*Ha* 3	*Shite*'s presentation (narration, dance)
	5	*Ha* 2	*Kyū*	*Shite* discloses identity, then leaves (*naka iri*)
Ai kyōgen interlude				
Second (*nochi ba*)	1	*Ha* 3	*Jo*	*Waki* waits for the *shite* to return
	2	*Ha* 3	*Ha* 1	*Shite* reappears in true form
	3	*Ha* 3	*Ha* 2	*Waki* and *shite* interact
	4	*Ha* 3	*Ha* 3	*Shite*'s presentation (narration, dance)
	5	*Kyū*	*Kyū*	Finale

the scene distinction and *jo-ha-kyū* progression within a model play. Model 1 represents Zeami's *dan* distinctions, considering *jo-ha-kyū* across both acts, while Model 2 identifies two distinct cycles of *jo-ha-kyū* in each act.[32]

This structure is not, however, universally applicable to all nō plays. An examination of the nō repertory demonstrates that each play has its own set of exceptions and distinctive traits, contributing to the variety found within the current repertory. *Mugen* plays tend to follow Zeami's model described above, but it is important to keep in mind that sections can be expanded, duplicated, contracted, or even omitted.

In *mugen* plays, the structure of the first and second act tend to mirror each other. Scene 1 centers on the *waki*, who causes the arrival of the *shite*. In Scene 2 the *shite* appears and chants solo, expressing their emotional state or current situation. In Scene 3, the distance (both physical and emotional) between *waki* and *shite* has shortened, and the two interact in a dialogue. Scene 4 is devoted to what can be called the *shite*'s "presentation." This is the core of each act, as attention is dedicated entirely to the *shite*, who tells a story by means of chant or dance. The *kuse* dance-narrative is usually found in this scene, either in Act 1 or Act 2, or sometimes in both. Act 2 Scene 4 often features a dance to instrumental music, and constitutes the climax of each act. From a narrative point of view, this is when the *shite* discloses core information about their identity, and when the background story is revealed. This is particularly important as many of these stories are based on patterns of concealment and revelation, described in more detail below.

The *ai kyōgen* interlude serves two main purposes. Narratively, it provides a respite after the first act's climax, helping the audience process the story, which is especially beneficial for those unfamiliar with the play's background. However, the use of explanatory materials in modern performances has lessened the importance of this function. Practically, the *ai kyōgen* offers a time interval, allowing the *shite* to change costume and mask before reentering in the second act.

Atsumori follows this structure, with the climax (Act 1, Scene 4) being a mimetic dance section to the accompaniment of chorus chant (*shimai*) in which various famous flutes are mentioned. Act 2 Scene 4 is the *kuse* mimetic dance sequence in which Atsumori describes the days spent at Ichinotani (see Figure 7 left), leading into the *chū no mai* dance (see Figure 7 right). The finale of the piece is the reenactment of Atsumori's last battle, ending with Naozane's pardon.

In *genzai* nō, the main characters are living humans, not spirits or deities. Consequently, it is not necessary to divide the play in two, with the *shite* exiting in the first act and reappearing in the second. The action is not solely focused on the *shite*, but often includes multiple characters who have similar importance in the development of the plot. It is therefore nearly impossible to present a "model structure" that applies to all plays in this category. Nonetheless, *genzai nō* draw on the same fundamental dramaturgical elements as *mugen nō*; thus similarities in the structure and progression of the story can be found. For example, plays begin with a journey, or with the arrival of a character at a certain location. The plot then progresses through the interaction of characters, often leading to a choreography scene, which could be a dance or a fight sequence. In the case of *Sumidagawa*, the *kakeri* dance occurs immediately after the entrance of the *shite*, but the play features numerous other highlights, such as the Miyako Birds sequence, the narration of the ferryman, who explains how the woman's son, Umewakamaru, died, the prayer scene, and the finale, with the mother trying to hug her son's ghost (see Figure 9 right).

The relationship between *shite* and *waki*

In essence, a nō play presents an episode centered around a key character, the *shite*, who encapsulates the theme of the story. Nō scholar Nogami Toyoichirō has famously described this as the "monodramatic principle" on which nō is based. The concept of "monodrama" suggests that plays are centered on the exploration of a single character, rather than on the action ensuing from the interaction between multiple characters. Nogami went as far as saying that drama "must have a conflict of personalities" but that "[a]s a rule, such conflict is absent in nō."[33]

Reading nō play texts, one realizes that, since they indeed feature more than one character, they are not "monodrama" in the strictest sense. Furthermore, if the action of the *shite* is prompted by their encounter with the *waki*, some degree of confrontation between these two roles must exist. Conflict may also be present strongly in other forms—that is, not necessarily personified by a character.

Auspicious plays from the first and fifth categories celebrate the harmonious coexistence of humans and deities, representing the minimum degree, if not complete absence, of confrontation. Most of the other plays, however, depict various forms of conflict, either in the past lives of the characters or in their present situation. For instance, in *Tadanori* (second category), the warrior-poet Taira no Tadanori, appearing as a ghost, complains that his poem was published anonymously because his clan lost the war. In *Kochō* (third category), the spirit of a butterfly laments being unable to enjoy the scent of plum blossoms, as this attachment prevents her from attaining enlightenment. In *Yuya*, the protagonist wishes to visit her dying mother but is compelled to accompany her lord to a flower-viewing party. In *Ataka* (fourth category), Benkei is torn between loyalty to his lord Yoshitsune and the need to humiliate him as a ploy to escape a dire situation.

"Drama" in nō primarily emerges from the encounters between the *shite* and *waki*, but rather than escalating into confrontation, these encounters typically evolve through rhetorical exchange. This progression moves from a state of mutual unawareness to one of shared understanding. This concept is encapsulated in the famous saying *ichiju no kage, ichiga no nagare*, meaning "to shelter under the same tree, to drink water from the same river," a phrase that symbolizes the interconnectedness of all beings through karma. It is significant that this expression is quoted in plays that explore meetings between strangers and delve into themes of nonduality, such as *Yamanba* and *Momijigari*.

In *mugen* plays, the spoken interaction between *shite* and *waki* reflects the dialectic nature of the Buddhist *mondō* "question and answer," in which teachings are conveyed through the dialogue between interlocutors, akin to the classical Greek *diálogos*. This interaction is crucial to the plot, with the *shite* and *waki* gradually growing closer, both emotionally and physically on stage, as the play progresses. The *waki*'s initial lack of knowledge allows the audience to relate and engage with the narrative through his perspective. In this kind of narrative, the *waki*'s role is not that of the antagonist, but one rather akin to a "sparring partner." In the nō *Atsumori*, too, the characters of Atsumori and Naozane resolve their conflict through their encounter. There are numerous other examples of story plots of this kind, with varying degrees of distance or antagonism between *shite* and *waki*, ultimately leading to resolution.

In *Sumidagawa*, the *shite* is not strongly contrasted by another character, but grapples with an internal conflict. The mother's inability to accept her son's loss drives her into derangement, initiating her journey toward the East. The development of the play is driven by her interaction with the Traveler and the Ferryman, who act as companions on her journey to resolution, encouraging her to join the people gathering around Umewakamaru's grave in reciting the *nenbutsu* prayer, and, finally, a reunion with her son's ghost. This ending seems to suggest that recovering from the profound trauma of losing a child is impossible. In other cases, the *waki*, too, may be suffering from an internal conflict, even though it is not rendered explicitly in the play. This is the case of genzai plays such as *Ataka*, in which Togashi initially prevents Yoshitsune and his men from crossing the barrier, but eventually relents and allows them to pass through.

Travel

In *mugen* nō the *waki* is typically a traveling priest, a mountain ascetic on a pilgrimage, or an imperial envoy, meeting the *shite* upon reaching his destination. However, the "journey" in nō is not just a "spatial journey" from one place to another but also a "temporal journey." Ghosts visit from the distant past to the present, as in the case of *Atsumori*, where Naozane travels from the Capital to Ichinotani, the place where he once killed Atsumori and where the ghost of the youth will appear to reenact their fatal encounter. The travel song mentioned earlier is a key moment of the play, referencing numerous famous locations on the way, thus helping the audience visualize the journey.

In *genzai* plays like *Sumidagawa*, the physical journey of the grieving mother along the Sumida River mirrors her emotional traversal through grief, despair, and hope for reunification with her lost child. While one of the characters travels, the other inhabits the location that is visited. Ghosts linger in places of significance due to powerful attachments, as in *Atsumori* or *Nonomiya*. Conversely, deities or demons may inhabit a location from time immemorial, as seen in *Momijigari* or *Takasago*.

Travel becomes a powerful narrative device, serving a dual purpose. On one hand, it acts as a metaphor for the human experience, symbolizing the individual's journey through life and death, here marked by the Buddhist notion of rebirth. On the other hand, it serves as a practical narrative expedient that facilitates the encounter of characters, often leading to pivotal plot developments. The *waki*, venturing into unknown lands, embodies a liminal figure, straddling the boundary between reality and fantasy, similar to the experience of the audience as it enters the world of the play.

Disguise and revelation

It is common for a single actor to act as *shite* in both acts of the same play, a tradition that likely originated as nō developed in the Muromachi period. This era saw the rise of highly acclaimed actors whose popularity led to the desire of both actors and audiences to have them appear in both roles.

This pattern of disguise and revelation of identity is recurrent in *mugen nō*.[34] For example, in *Atsumori* the *shite* appears in the first act as one of the grass cutters, but later reveals himself to be the ghost of Atsumori. Zeami noted that "plays divided into two parts and where [the atmosphere] changes, are easy to write. In plays performed without a break, one should write parts that look different. This is important. If this is lacking, it will be monotonous and bad."[35] It is not surprising that Zeami, who was much concerned with the audience's reception of his art, penned a great number of *mugen* plays. In contrast, the living characters depicted in *genzai nō*, such as in *Sumidagawa*, do not undergo transformation. In that play, the *shite* consistently depicts a mother who is deeply devoted to her child and who maintains her role and emotional state throughout the narrative.[36]

Japanese literature scholar Nose Asaji (1894–1955) called plays in which the *shite* reveals their identity in the second act *kegen* plays (avatar plays), where *kegen* is the "embodiment" or "incarnation" of a supernatural being. The Japanese word *kegen* refers to the avatar of a Buddha appearing in this world to bring people to salvation. Numerous stories in Buddhist scriptures and discourses feature deities who manifest in the world in human form. Additionally, there are folk tales where animals such as foxes, raccoons, or cranes transform into humans to interact with people. This element of *kegen* could be a remnant from when nō was predominantly a religious drama, or it may have been influenced by folk culture. Rebirth is a fundamental concept in Buddhist philosophy, where past actions, influenced by karma, determine future existences, potentially including nonhuman forms. Entities that appear human might be incarnations of wandering spirits, striving to escape the cycle of rebirth and find enlightenment.

Nō scholar Tashiro Keiichirō (1930–2014) noted that the first act in *mugen* plays is a spatial detachment from reality, in which the *waki* is drawn into the dream space, and the second act is a temporal detachment from the present, in which the *waki* is taken back through skillful narration to a time when the *shite* once existed. Hence, the *mae shite* could be interpreted as an alter ego sent as a messenger (*tsukai*) rather than an embodiment of the *nochi shite*.[37]

There are also several plays in which characters are possessed by gods or spirits that transmit oracles, and also by ghosts. Once possessed, the person's body is unable to control itself. For example, in *Futari Shizuka* (*Two Shizukas*), a village girl picking new shoots for New Year rituals near a river is possessed by the ghost of Shizuka Gozen, the skilled dancer who was once the lover of Minamoto no Yoshitsune. In the second act, the village girl possessed by the ghost of Shizuka appears again, but next to her materializes the ghost of Shizuka herself. The two Shizukas (*shite* and *tsure*) wear the same type of costume and dance the same dance, coordinating their movements. In this way a single character is split into two, possessor and possessed.

The idea of the same entity manifesting as different beings aligns with the fluid concept of identity in Shintō and Buddhist philosophies, reflecting the social perspectives of the era in which these plays were written. It is important to recognize that disguise in this context does not mean deception; rather, it serves as a manifestation of the inherent complexity and multifaceted nature of existence itself.

The prevalence of the pattern of disguise and revelation in nō can also be attributed to its fundamental appeal in dramaturgy. At first, the stage presents itself as an empty space, and then, gradually, elements emerge into view. This act of concealing and showing objects is perhaps the most primordial form of performative action. In the context of nō, where only one main character appears in each play, this pattern allows for the presence of two distinct entities on stage, each with unique costumes and masks.

Moreover, the revelation itself can be executed in compelling ways. For example, a character may hide in a stage property and then reappear in a different guise. Even in *Sumidagawa*, where the *shite* maintains the same identity throughout the play, the mother first appears wearing a travel hat, but then removes it to show her face, thus adding an element of change and visual interest (see Figures 8 and 9). Finally, the process of revelation can be perceived as a transition from "ignorance" to "knowledge," which is particularly evident in *mugen* plays where the audience views the narrative through the lens of the "ignorant" *waki*. As we journey with the *waki*, our discovery of the hidden identity of the *shite* character constructs a compelling narrative arc that sustains interest. This technique effectively maintains audience engagement even when the plot is familiar, transcending mere suspense and resonating with the timeless appeal of compelling storytelling.

Narration

Actors in nō performances can be said to embody their characters inasmuch as they engage in action and dialogue that drives the plot. However, nō plays also feature extended sections of apparent "non-action," in which actors chant while remain relatively still (See Chapter 3 Movement). One key example is the *nanori* sequence in which the *waki*, or sometimes the *shite*, introduce themselves, directly addressing the audience. For example, in *Atsumori* Renshō begins his *nanori* as follows: "You have before you one who in his time was Kumagai Jirō Naozane, a warrior from Musashi province." *Nanori* may be followed by a travel song, where characters recount their journey (past or ongoing), while standing still. Renshō's travel song to Ichinotani (about seventy kilometers from Kyoto) in *Atsumori* reads as follows:

> The wandering moon,
> Issuing from among the Ninefold Clouds [...]
> swings southward by Yodo and Yamazaki,
> past Koya Pond and the Ikuta River, [Mimes walking.]
> and Suma shore, loud with pounding waves,
> to Ichi-no-tani, where I have arrived

Two points should be made. First, although these passages might be considered "non-action" from a choreographic perspective (the performer is, for the most part, motionless), they still constitute "action" in terms of producing an effect that alters the situation and advances the plot.[38] In these play sections nō characters seem to morph into "secondary narrators," in contrast with the "primary narrator," typically an external voice.[39] While in literature the shift from primary to secondary narrator is common, nō lacks a hierarchy of voices. The story emerges from the characters themselves, who sometimes even relate their actions as they unfold in the dramatic "present tense," and through the chorus, who most of the time narrates on their behalf.[40] It would not be an overstatement to say that the narratorial and mimetic components of nō are equally important. Here is an interesting example from Atsumori:

> YOUTH (*sashi*) Those who gather grass on yonder hill
> now start from home, for twilight is at hand.
> YOUTH AND COMPANIONS They too head back to
> Suma, by the sea,
> And their way, like mine, is hardly long.
> Back and forth I ply, from hill to shore,
> Heart heavy with the cares of thankless toil.

Atsumori and his companions, appearing as grass cutters, act as narrators, describing the seafolk of Suma returning home after work (see Figure 6). The passage plays into the fact that Atsumori, too, when he was alive, was forced to live like a grass cutter, as his clan was escaping to the West. Although the *shite* here is talking about grass cutters in Suma (the way he appears now before the *waki*), he is also talking about his past self. Again, in *Sumidagawa*, shortly after her entrance, the mother sings:

> WOMAN [...] This I know well, now I roam, astray
> The highroads, among the travelers.

How can I tell them, how shall I seek
the place where my son has gone?
[...]
WOMAN Frail the dew on Makuzu Moor,
CHORUS and I as frail, am I to live on,
Even bitter at my lot?
WOMAN I lived for many years at Kita-Shirakawa, in the northern district of Miyako. One day, alas, disaster struck, for my only son,
enticed away by traders in children,
vanished from my side.

In this passage the woman and the chorus share a single narrative in which the mother describes her situation. Here we see nō theatre's roots in the rich storytelling traditions that predate it.[41] This aspect of nō is somehow akin to ancient Greek Homeric epic poetry, that involved both indirect storytelling and moments in which the reader would utter lines in the first person, "pretending to be" a certain character. However, at least since Plato and Aristotle, drama has been thought to focus on the mimetic element in which actors fictionalize the narrative by imitating the actions and utterances of the distinct characters.[42] The nineteenth-century interpretation of theatre realism maximized this idea, removing the "fourth wall" to create an effect of verisimilitude. It is no coincidence that, since the twentieth century, nō has served as a source of inspiration for playwrights seeking to break free from the constraints of Western naturalism.[43]

The chorus

Nō plays begin with characters reciting monologues, then progress to dialogues. As the plot advances, the chorus joins the recitation. The presence of the chorus has often led to comparisons between nō and ancient Greco-Roman theatre. However, while the chorus in the latter has a defined role as a character, mediator, or narrator, its role in nō is less clear and open to interpretation. This is partly because the linguistic cues often do not explicitly indicate the perspective or "voice" being represented. In numerous instances the chorus's voice can be associated with either the *shite* or the *waki*.[44]

These aspects of the text enhance the sense of nō as an act of "collective narration," in which every performer partakes in the communal representation of a story, thereby blurring the lines between roles.[45] Indeed, in Zeami's time the lines assigned to the chorus in contemporary practice were together sung by the chorus, *shite*, *waki*, and *tsure* characters, with the *waki* acting as chorus leader. The distinction between individual roles and the chorus appears to have emerged later.[46] Consider the next passage from the second half of *Atsumori*:

> RENSHŌ for we, once enemies
> ATSUMORI are now become
> RENSHŌ in very truth
> ATSUMORI fast friends in the Law.
> CHORUS Now I understand! 'Leave the company of an evil friend, cleave to the foe you judge a good man': and that good man is you! O I am grateful! How can I thank you as you deserve? Then I will make confession of my tale, and pass the night recounting it to you.[47]

One single line flows from Renshō to Atsumori, and then to the chorus. This is a recurrent rhetorical pattern, emphasizing the proximity of the two characters and the overlapping of their thoughts.[48] It is all the more intriguing to consider that, in ancient nō practices, the chorus lines, which can easily be attributed to Atsumori, would have been led by the *waki*, in this case Renshō. If the premise of nō performance is that there is no full "suspension of disbelief," so that each play is a narration or presentation, rather than an attempt at reproducing events as they unfolded, then all performers can be considered as being detached from the text at different levels. In addition to musicians and chorus members, who are clearly separated from the "fiction" of the reproduction of a character, the actors too, though sometimes identifying with the role, may be seen as "stepping out of character" and reciting as if they were external narrators. A similar disconnection between actor and role can be seen in movement (see Chapter 3, Movement).

Genzai plays typically feature longer exchanges between characters, hence the chorus parts may be shorter. In these plays, the chorus often seems to be describing the actions of the *shite* as if it were acting as an external narrator.[49] For example, at the end of *Sumidagawa*, while the chorus sing the following passage, *shite* and *kokata* act out the scene on stage in a realistic manner (see Figure 9 right).

> She takes his hand, his slips into hers,
> but again his shape fades and is gone.
> [...]
> What seemed a dear child is wild grasses
> thick on the tomb, nodding in sign
> over wide, grassy wastes,
> O sorrow: nothing else remains[50]

Literary characteristics

Nō plays draw from a broad spectrum of sources, encompassing virtually the entire history of Japanese literature up to the period in which they were composed. These include chronicles of myths (e.g., *Kojiki*, early 8th century), poetry collections (e.g., *Man'yōshu*, 7th-8th century, *Kokin wakashū*, 10th century), novels (e.g., *Tale of Genji*, 11th century), military tales (e.g., *The Tale of the Heike*, 13th century), as well as religious texts. In addition, several commentaries on these ancient sources had already been written by the time nō emerged, and these too were utilized by playwrights.

The story of Atsumori and Naozane (Renshō) is told in Volume IX of *The Tale of the Heike*, with Naozane as the main character. This is one of the most famous as well as moving episodes of the chronicle. In the play, it is not fully enacted by the actors, but it is told by the *ai kyōgen*. In the original story, Naozane confronts Atsumori and throws him to the ground in the heat of battle. Preparing to deliver the final blow, Naozane hesitates as he realizes that Atsumori is only 16 years old—the same age as his own son. Urged by Atsumori to end his life quickly, Naozane is torn. The other Minamoto warriors are approaching, and they may be less merciful to Atsumori's body. Understanding the grim necessity of his action, in tears, he kills Atsumori and respectfully takes his head. Only then does he discover a flute on Atsumori's body and realizes that the haunting music he heard coming from the Taira camp the night before was played by him. Afterwards, realizing the fleeting nature of life, Naozane embraces Buddhism and is ordained a monk, taking the name Renshō.

Nō characters express themselves through poetry, and Atsumori, a character sensitive to the arts and skilled in music and dance, makes an ideal protagonist from Zeami's perspective. Whether they are grass cutters, courtiers, village women, or high priests, they can all quote verses by heart and engage in poetic conversations with each other, creating layers of semantic overtones. *Waka*, the most popular form of Japanese classical poetry, consisting of five lines of five and seven syllables, greatly influenced the way nō plays were composed. The language of nō is replete with rhetorical devices borrowed from *waka*, such as "pivot words" (*kakekotoba*) in which the phonetic reading of characters suggests multiple meanings, often used to link verses, or other poetic techniques that aim to trigger associations between place names, natural elements, and human emotions, thus creating complex intertextual and intratextual overtones.[51] The inclusion of famous *waka* in imperial anthologies, such as the *Kokin wakashū*, allowed for a specific vocabulary to become canonical and widespread, influencing other arts, including nō. Knowledge of these devices provides access to this otherwise invisible web of literary references.

Celebrated from an early age for his extraordinary talent in linked verse poetry, Zeami brought this expertise into his nō compositions. In his treatises, he urged the author to think about what kind of language would be appropriate for a certain character and choose expressions of congratulation, lamentation, or love, using relevant quotes from literary materials.[52] In *Sandō*, he noted that "a play should have a place where the original source is pointed out. If it is an evocative and famous place or a legendary site, then you should take lines from well-known poems about the place, in Chinese or Japanese, and write them into concentrated points in the three *dan* of *ha*."[53] Zeami's approach to playwriting focuses on the *shite*, carefully selecting expressions that resonate with audiences, which helps to achieve the thematic coherence of the entire play.

Every nō play is located in specific locations, often temples, shrines, or natural landmarks like mountains or shores. These places can be so relevant as to become the play's title, as in *Ataka* (*The Ataka Barrier*), *Ōeyama* (Mt. Ōe), or *Nonomiya* (*The Shrine in the Field*). Playwrights choose their locations from existing stories featuring famous locations (*meisho*) inscribed in poetry anthologies. The mere mention of such locations allows the audience to evoke not only a story but also an emotion that connotes these places. This is a literary device known as *utamakura*. It is clear that medieval audiences possessed a deep understanding of these references, which were acquired through songs, legends, and poetry.[54] The influence of such tropes was so strong as to influence later arts, to an extent that is recognizable by an educated, contemporary audience.

Beyond merely serving as geographic locations, settings in nō plays are deeply infused with seasonal imagery and emotional undertones. For instance, a play might capture the springtime splendor of cherry blossoms at Mt. Yoshino or the autumnal hues of red leaves at Mt. Tatsuta. These settings are emotionally charged, associating the renewal of spring at places like Kiyomizu Temple in *Tamura* with the transient beauty of cherry blossoms, or the reflective melancholy of autumn at Suma Bay. Spring and autumn dominate the thematic landscape of nō, mirroring their prevalence in traditional poetry collections due to their climatic appeal, with fewer plays set in the harsher seasons of summer and winter. Examples include *Kamo*, a summer play with motifs of refreshing water scenes, and *Hachinoki*, a winter play that begins amidst a snowstorm in Sano, using white cotton wool to depict a snow-laden potted tree. This careful matching of the play's setting with its seasonal staging enhances the connection between the audience and the play's world, crafting a cohesive time–space experience on stage.[55]

The origin of the story of Umewakamaru in *Sumidagawa* is unclear, though it is now memorialized by a temple near the Sumida River, suggesting it may have developed from the nō, or possibly existed as an oral tradition prior to being recorded. Sumida River itself is, however, a real location. Flowing through modern-day Tokyo (Edo), and far from the ancient capital of Kyoto (Miyako), it became widely recognized through a famous poem in the *Kokin wakashū* that expresses the longing and concern of lovers who are apart. The poem is quoted by the mother as she approaches the riverbank.

WOMAN […] Are you true to your name?
Then, Miyako birds,
I put you this question:
the one I love –
does she live or does she die?[56]

She then notices white birds with red feet and beaks—a breed unknown in the capital. When she inquiries about them, the ferryman calls them "gulls," but the woman urges him to call them "Miyako-dori" (Miyako birds, or "birds from the capital"), thus referencing the poem. However, the madwoman then clarifies that her longing is for her child, not the lover mentioned in the poem. The chant continues with other quotes from the poem collection *Tales of Ise* and ends with a plea to be taken aboard a ship, reflecting her deep yearning for her child.

The setting of *Atsumori* is Ichinotani in Suma Bay, where Atsumori meets his demise. Located in today's Hyōgo Prefecture, Suma was historically viewed as a remote exile site, far from the capital, Kyoto. This place became an *utamakura* for solitude and desolation. Suma is mentioned in court poet Ariwara no Yukihira's lament in the *Kokin wakashū*, and in *The Tale of Genji*.[57] These cultural and emotional associations are integral to *Atsumori*, aligning with its narrative and enhancing the play's thematic depth, which the audience is expected to recognize.

The *kuse* dance-narrative section is also replete with poetic devices. The chorus describes the miserable life of the Taira as they were chased out of the capital and forced to take refuge in such a remote place.

> ATSUMORI While winds swept down upon us off the hills
> CHORUS The fields were bitterly cold.
> At the sea's edge
> our ships huddled close, while day and night
> the plovers cried
> and our own poor sleeves
> wilted in the spray that drenched the beach.[58]

The poem vividly portrays the harsh nature of Suma Bay, simultaneously serving as a metaphor for the emotions of the Taira clansmen. This is conveyed through the sophisticated use of homophones, a distinctive feature of the Japanese language. Below is a transcription of the romanized Japanese text, following the seven–five syllable meter with the exception of lines 1 and 5 (eight syllables). To the right is a literal translation of each word, presented in the order they appear.

SHITE

1.	u shi ro/no/ya ma/ka ze	[behind/of/the hills/wind]
2.	fu ki/o chi te	[swept/down]

CHORUS

3.	no/mo/sa e/ka e ru	[the fields/too/being cold/ bitterly]
4.	u mi/gi wa/ni	[the sea/edge/at]
5.	fu ne/no/yo ru/to/naku	[ships/are/huddled close/too/ not]
6.	hi ru/to/na ki	[day/too/not]
7.	chi do ri/no/ko e/mo	[the plovers/of/voice/too]
8.	wa ga/so de/mo	[my/sleeves/too]
9.	na mi/ni/shi wo ru ru	[waves/by/drenched]
10.	I so ma ku ra	[seashore pillow]

In writing, these words are expressed, as usual in Japanese through a combination of *kanji* (Chinese ideograms) and *kana* (phonetic syllabic writing), thereby rendering a specific meaning explicit. However, their phonetic rendering opens the meaning to multiple interpretations.[59] In line 2, *ochite* has a double meaning: the wind blowing "down" from the mountains on the Suma coast and the Taira clan's "escape" from the capital to Suma. In line 3, *kaeru* carries a triple meaning: a "bitterly" cold wind, migratory plovers "returning" to the sea, and going "back" to the boats being pursued by the enemy. In line 5, *yoru* refers both to the ships "huddling close" and to "night," contrasting with *hiru* ("day") in the following line. In line 9, *nami* can be interpreted in three ways: the "waves," the "cry" of the plovers, and the "tears" shed by the Taira clansmen.

Weakened and frightened by the imminent enemy attack, the Taira cluster together like birds shivering with cold and weeping loudly, their feathers soaked with water, here represented by their sleeves. In classical poetry, wet sleeves are usually associated with tears, further reinforcing the image of the Taira's desperation. The reference to sleeves also refers to sleep, as the term used is *isomakura* (lit. "seashore pillow"), evoking images of uncomfortable sleep while traveling to distant lands. After this passage, the chorus goes on to sing about how the Taira slept in the thatched huts of fishermen, and mentions the smoke from cooking fires, which also reminds them of the smoke from salt kilns. This is a reference to *The Tale of Genji*, in which tells how Prince Genji had to live in exile at Suma. This overlap of poetic images exemplifies Zeami's teaching that there should be a coherence of poetic images, with quotations of well-known poems relevant to the scene. This passage illustrates the intricate use of poetic language in nō texts. Understanding and interpreting these devices enable a richer and more profound emotional connection with the text.

3

Performance

Everything that happens on a nō stage is meticulously choreographed. From the orderly entrance of the chorus and musicians to the synchronized way stage assistants (*kōken*) place or remove a property at the beginning and end of a play, no gesture is casual, nothing is left to chance. This principle of restraint and coordination originates in the court etiquette that influenced nō when performers were required to appear before aristocrats in highly formal situations. The method of moving around the stage using the sliding step (*suriashi*) that is so characteristic of nō is also used in other arts that originated in the Muromachi period, such as tea ceremony, and derives from the way cultured people walked inside buildings. Other habits, such as sitting with folded legs (*seiza*) and wearing *montsuki* (a black silk crested kimono) and *hakama* (divided skirt) were influenced by samurai culture in the Edo period. All participants in a performance maintain a uniform, emotionally neutral facial expression throughout the performance. This behavior may be seen as a formalized, perhaps radicalized, expression of a general Japanese *habitus* of physical control in formal situations.[1] In the case of nō, this comportment has the important value of preventing the breaking of concentration of both the audience and the actors or drawing attention away from the focus of the performance.

The guiding aesthetics and practical principles underlying all aspects of nō performance are rooted in minimalism, emphasizing efficacy. Anything deemed unnecessary is omitted. The performance is stripped down to the bare minimum, thus rendering the few elements that are left strongly charged with meaning, and what may appear as limitations do not detract from the emotional resonance of the play. Joy, sorrow, illusion, hope, romance—a broad spectrum of human emotions are evoked by the performance.

Elements such as stage design, movement, music, the use of costumes and masks, all of this incorporates *ma* (間), a term signifying a gap, pause, or blank. In this aesthetic of incompletion, empty spaces provide fertile ground where the audience's imagination is actively engaged. The deliberate omission of elements leads to a more abstract expression of the characters and the narratives they portray.

In literature, indeterminacy arises in the communication between the text and reader, where the text is neither identical to the reality it represents nor to the reader's perspective. This indeterminacy serves as a catalyst, shaping the reader's interpretation of the text.[2] The same theory may be applied to watching a performance. In nō, this may initially be difficult to embrace. However, once accepted, it becomes a liberating element, enabling each spectator to engage with the incomplete forms presented on stage and to form a personal interpretation of the plays.

The characters and stories draw from known historical or literary sources that shape the audience's expectations of their portrayal. Over the centuries, such narratives have evolved through collective imagination. Therefore, characters are not created anew when watching a performance but are accompanied by discourses that have been associated with them over time.[3] Yet this plurality of notions does not result in the creation of a defined or exact depiction of a character. Rather, the audience builds on pre-existent knowledge to develop multiple, diverse forms of reception.

Stage

Nō was originally performed on makeshift stages or within existing structures such as the pavilions of temples and shrines. The form of the nō stage we recognize today was perfected at the end of the sixteenth century, and its architecture has remained largely unchanged since.[4] While seemingly simple in appearance, the nō stage is defined by a multitude of features that carry both practical and symbolic significance. Stages are built with *hinoki* cypress wood, and they are constructed with traditional techniques, without the use of nails. The main stage (*hon butai*) consists of a square main stage of approximately 5.4 × 5.4 meters, one meter high, and covered with a thatched roof made of tree bark that is supported by four pillars (see Figure 1 and 2). Additional platforms are attached to the back of the stage (*ato za*) where musicians and stage assistants sit, and to stage left (*jiutai za*) where the chorus sits.

The *ato za* is connected stage right to a passageway (*hashigakari*, or "connecting bridge") typically stretching 11 to 13 meters in length and slightly tilted toward the curtain (*age maku*). Three small pine trees stand in front of the *hashigakari*, their heights gradually decreasing as they approach the curtain. This creates an illusion of depth, making the curtain appear farther away. The pine trees also act as reference points for actors who often pause there to deliver chant. While most of the action takes place on the main stage, the *hashigakari* is not a mere passage point, but is also used as a performance area, for example to signify a separate location from that represented on the main stage.

As nō scholar Miyamoto Keizō put it, "nō begins and ends with walking."[5] The presence of the *hashigakari* requires anyone entering or exiting the stage across it to parade horizontally before the audience. The *hashigakari* has the metaphorical value of connecting two existential dimensions: that of reality/present, inhabited by the *waki* and by extension the audience, and that of fiction/past, from where the *shite* appear. The *shite* briefly visits to narrate their story before departing, leaving no trace, until they are summoned again.

The *hashigakari* extends into the "mirror room" (*kagami no ma*), a space behind the curtain from where characters and musicians enter and exit. As the name suggests, this room is fitted with mirrors that are used to complete the preparations for the *shite* before they go on stage. The only other entrance to the stage is the *kirido-guchi*, a small sliding door at upstage left. A depiction of bamboo, known for its rapid growth and resilience, is often painted where the *kirido-guchi* is. At the other end of the stage, the curtain features five vertical colored panels: purple, white, red, yellow, and green.[6] These colors reflect the Chinese theory of the five elements, which represent the universe. Indeed, the idea that the curtain is a gateway to the infinite is very evocative. Similar curtains are also used in Buddhist temples, suggesting that their use in nō may be a remnant from the time when performances were held in temple settings. The use of this type of curtain dates back at least to the time of Zeami, who mentions it in his writings.[7]

Besides the *hashigakari*, one of the most iconic features of the nō stage is the painting of an old pine tree on the *kagami ita* ("mirror board") at the back (see Figure 1). The symbolism of the pine tree in nō has various interpretations and is deeply rooted in traditional beliefs, in which trees are considered the dwelling places of deities. The pine, with its evergreen foliage symbolizing enduring vitality, is held in particular reverence. This may be a remnant of nō theatre's origins as a votive performance, when stages were set up facing a sacred object, often a tree, with the audience viewing the performance from behind. The pine on the "mirror board" may be seen as "reflecting" this sacred tree, which would have been positioned where the audience sits today. While this interpretation lacks definitive historical evidence, it provides a compelling connection to the early history of nō. More broadly, both pine and bamboo are considered auspicious elements frequently found in decorative wall paintings; in nō, they evoke the natural outdoor environment where nō performances originated.

Another such reminder is the strip of white pebbles (*shirasu*) that runs around the wooden structure. Old stages used to have white gravel cover the area where the audience sits today.[8] Important patrons would watch from separate buildings, while the populace would stand or sit on the ground. One theory has it that this area may have been intended as a lighting device, as the sun's rays would be reflected on it to illuminate the stage, perhaps replicating the effect of water surrounding stages such as the one at Itsukushima Shrine in Miyajima (Hiroshima Prefecture). The white *shirasu* may instead have had the symbolic purpose of repelling impurities (*kegare*) to maintain the "sanctity" of the stage.

Although nō performers have no religious authority, they embody characters such as deities or spirits that are manifested through the masks they wear. The highly ritualized representation of these characters may create a sense of awe and respect among participants. This effect is accentuated by the design of the stage, which resembles an altar upon which supernatural beings are summoned before the audience across the *hashigakari*, and ceremoniously sent back at the end of the performance.

Indeed, the nō stage, like any performance space, is a highly liminal space, serving as a threshold not only between the audience and performers but also among all participants and the characters depicted in the story.[9] It also represents a junction between the present (the audience) and the past (the characters and stories summoned on stage). Several elements contribute to this sense of liminality, among which are the roofed structure set within a theatre hall, consistent lighting on both stage and auditorium throughout the performance, and the closeness of audience seats to the performers. The stage, embraced by the audience on two sides, creates a palpable sense of "togetherness." This feeling is reinforced by the absence of a curtain covering the stage, making all cast visible throughout the performance (see Figure 1).

Additionally, the *kizahashi* staircase connects the front of the stage with the seating area. Historically, performance organizers used this staircase to access the stage and prepare for the commencement of the performance. Today, it is no longer used for this purpose and seldom serves as part of the stage area. However, the staircase may be seen as a symbolic access point to the stage, further reinforcing its liminal nature.

The *hinoki* cypress used to build the stage is a natural choice, since it is also used for shrines and other traditional buildings. It is usually forbidden to step on it without wearing the white *tabi* (split-toed socks) used by nō performers. Since *tabi* are only put on just before the performance and removed after the show, this ensures that the surface is not damaged and retains its shine, an important requirement as the actors must be able to slide across it. The stage needs to be polished periodically to keep the wood from drying out.

The long, flexible stage planks run the length of the square stage, creating the feeling of walking on a drumhead, where normal walking produces audible sounds as opposed to the silence of a sliding step. This acoustic feature is further enhanced by several earthen jars strategically placed under the stage at certain angles, intended to amplify the sounds produced by foot stamps, a feature of nō dance that is said to originate in the tradition of chasing away evil spirits or awakening positive energies (*henbai*).[10]

The architectural design of the stage includes elements essential to navigating the space. Since the actors are often masked and thus have limited visibility of the stage floor, they rely on the tactile feedback of their feet sliding along the gaps at the joints between the planks for orientation. Other important space markers are the columns that support the stage roof. While these pillars can sometimes obstruct the audience's view, they are crucial for actors wearing masks. Due to the limited field of vision, actors are in real danger of falling off the stage. The *metsuke-bashira* ("sighting pillar") downstage right is of the greatest importance, as it marks the outermost boundary of the stage, the one closest to the audience on both sides. The area near this pillar, called *sumi* ("corner"), is where many of the highlights of a piece of choreography take place.

The main stage space is commonly conceived as being divided into nine equally sized sectors, named after their positioning or function: *jō za* ("standard place," also called *nanori za*, as characters often deliver the *nanori* self-introduction while standing there); *daishō mae* (in front of the large and small drums); *fue za mae* (in front of the flute); *jiutai za mae* (in front of the chorus); *waki za mae* (in front of the *waki*); *shōsaki* (center front); *sumi* (corner); *waki shōmen* (side front); *shōnaka* (center). Over time, such areas have begun to be labeled with specific names that are useful for teaching and studying the choreography of a play.

One might wonder, however, whether the nō stage developed its architectural features to facilitate performance, or if it was the performers who adapted to it? The interplay between the physical attributes of the stage and the action of the performer is so deep that it is difficult to determine which influenced the other—whether it was the design of the stage that shaped the movement, or vice versa.[11] It has already been pointed out that, although the fundamental elements of nō were established toward the end of the sixteenth century (see Chapter 1, Developments), its performance techniques have continued to change over its long history. For example, the *suriashi* sliding step is closely related to the development of *tabi* as indoor footwear in the late Muromachi period and early Edo period.[12] It is reasonable to think that, before the diffusion of *tabi*, actors used to perform barefoot, or perhaps with some kind of footwear.[13] The introduction of *tabi*, allowing the feet to slide smoothly on wooden surfaces, must have strongly influenced this basic component of nō movement. In addition, the geometric configuration of the square stage, open on two sides, inherently influenced choreographies, which typically feature circular movements or linear progressions that follow the diagonal axes of the stage. These patterns are chosen over purely horizontal movements to ensure that the depth of the square stage is fully exploited.

Movement

Those who experience nō plays are often impressed by the long, static sections of a play that primarily involve the delivery of text through chanting, occasionally accompanied by music. During these segments, the characters usually stand or sit facing the audience, while sometimes the chorus sings in place of the actors. The actor's immobility is justified by the need to foreground the chanted word to emphasize the beauty of the poetic text and the meanings it evokes through the musicality of the voice. As the story progresses and the dramatic tension escalates, the physical actions of the *shite*, who is at once actor and narrator, increasingly complement the verbal expression.

Movements do not accompany the entire text but are used to emphasize only certain passages, thus enriching the narrative with visual and kinetic elements. The long moments of immobility effectively set the stage for action scenes: Against a background of stillness, even the slightest movement of the head or arm is easily noticed and given meaning. Zeami famously wrote that actors should move ten parts of the mind, and seven parts of the body, as "this will surely produce interest and excitement."[14] This principle is still applied today. Following the choreography, nō actors limit their movements, thus creating kinetic "blanks" to be filled by the imagination of the audience. In all of this restraint and limitation, how do performers adapt the forms to "act" a character?

Although movement forms are prescribed by tradition, they are not singular or absolute. The angle at which the knees should be bent, the height at which a hand should be held, the number of steps required to reach a certain position on stage—virtually every part of movement is subject to interpretation by the individual performer. While the *iemoto* embodies the style that represents a school (*ryūgi*), other actor families within the same school may perform slightly different variations of the model. Such variations may appear slight to the untrained eye but are quite obvious to the expert spectator.

The very existence of a prescribed norm is what allows for exceptions and deviations to emerge. Even though the repetition of a limited choreographic vocabulary may seem to tend toward uniformity, what it really produces is variation.[15] This is one of the great pleasures of nō: Once the audience has developed a knowledge of the basic performance conventions, it is possible to notice and appreciate a vast number of differences.

It may be useful to consider two types of adaptation of nō forms: "adapting to the character" and "adapting to the self." Movements are modified to suit different types of characters. Typically, nō characters correspond to role-types, such as the "old man," the "crazed woman," the "Taira warrior," and so on. A certain degree of role-type categorization already existed in the early Muromachi period. In his treatises, Zeami mentions three styles that the actor should master: the Aged Mode (*rōtai*), the Woman's Mode (*nyotai*), and the Martial Mode (*guntai*).[16] In recent times, other categorizations have been suggested.[17] These role-types refer not only to their plot function but also to how the characters are represented in performance, including through movement and chant, as well as aspects such as masks, costumes, and choreography. Different role-types require different *kamae* (posture) and *hakobi* (style of walking). For example, court ladies appear smaller, with feet in line and hands close to the waist, forming a small arm circle, and taking small steps—this may also result from the costume they are wearing, which restricts leg movement. Strong characters such as warriors or demons keep their feet and hands wide apart, with an even lower center of gravity and a broader stride. These latter roles often stand in a *kamae* type called *hanmi* (half body), similar to the stance in martial arts, with one foot and hand pointing forward and the other to the side.

In addition to this formal type of adaptation, some actors strive to "act the character" by further personalizing or interpreting it, believing that merely adapting to a role-type would make the performance dull or predictable. Yet, since nō is essentially based on forms, other actors focus on perfect execution, and for them individual interpretation is to the detriment of the abstraction that is required to create the fertile blank to be filled by the audience's imagination.

Movements are also adapted to the "self," that is to the physicality of the individual who executes them. Over time, actors refine their style, adapting posture, walk, and gesture to their preferences and responding to the natural evolution of their bodies. As performers age, their physical capabilities naturally change, leading to necessary adaptations in their style. This evolution of the physique is generally accepted as a natural part of the process. While it is difficult to generalize, it is often observed that, as performers gain years and experience, their style tends to simplify. With mastery, actors can achieve more profound results with fewer gestures. The ephemerality of embodied knowledge, to include both dance and musical expressions such as chant, makes it so that such a form mutates with time, as well as with the corporeality of individuals that embody it.

It is worth clarifying that, in a broad sense, all that pertains to movement in nō is referred to as being *mai* (dance). In a narrower sense, however, *mai* refers to specific sequences involving continuous movement across the stage: This includes dance with instrumental music (*mai* and *hataraki*) and narrative dance with chant (*shimai*), which are described in more detail below.

Posture (*kamae*)

Kamae, the posture that is the beginning and the end of all movement sequences, is maintained throughout the performance, whether the actor is standing, sitting, or moving. Basic *kamae* differs from school to school, but it generally requires bending the knees, keeping the chest upright, straightening the neck, and keeping the chin tucked in.[18] The arms form an oval with the elbows pointing outward and the fingers in the shape of an elongated fist with the index finger curled around the extended thumb. *Kamae* ensures that no part of the body is left casually idle.

Bending the knees lowers the center of gravity. This helps to maintain a stable posture and prevent unintentional wobbling when walking. *Koshi o ireru* ("be aware of the pelvis and straighten one's posture") is an expression often used in training as a key point for creating good *kamae*. The nō performer's body appears to be rooted to the floor. This is in contrast to Western styles of dance such as ballet, in which the dancer's body is raised off the floor. A key purpose of *kamae* is that of providing support for the costume, which typically feature large and ornate sleeves that can only be fully visible when the actor keeps the arms detached from the torso. Pulling in the chin brings the mask closer to the body, creating a more compact figure.

Kamae is neither action nor rest. It is a position of constant readiness. Actors with good *kamae* are praised for emanating what may be called "stage presence." More an effect than a quality of the actor, nō stage presence can be seen as arising from the contrast between the actor's "ordinary" existence, perceived through visible body parts such as the chin and hands, and slight movements caused by breathing or singing, and the "extraordinary" stillness of *kamae*, which actors must hold for the duration of the performance.

Walking (*hakobi*)

One of the most recognizable features of nō is the unique way the characters move across the stage by bending their knees and sliding their feet. The act of walking is referred to as *hakobi* while feet-sliding is *suriashi*. Walking is done with great control, regardless of the speed or intensity of the movement. White *tabi* have a reinforced sole that allows for smooth movement, and their whiteness draws attention to the feet.

This distinctive style of movement produces several effects. First, since *hakobi* relies solely on the legs and feet while the upper body remains as motionless as possible, it creates an otherworldly effect. With their bodies clad in elaborate costumes and their faces covered by masks, nō characters resemble living statues sliding over the stage surface. Together with *kamae*, the control of the gait makes it possible to perform defined movements that appear even more powerful. This technique prevents the mask, which is particularly sensitive to tilting, from altering its expression during movements sequences.

When sliding their feet, the performers keep their toes pressed down as they move forward. This movement is momentarily interrupted as they lift their toes slightly just before the foot settles, while the opposing foot begins to move. Although this toe lifting may seem spontaneous, it is actually a deliberate action. Lifting the toes marks the end of one step and the beginning of another, turning even the basic act of walking into a point of interest. As the pace increases, the heels naturally rise. Keeping the entire surface of the sole in constant contact with the ground would result in stilted movements.

Choreographic patterns (*kata*)

In the context of movement, the term *kata* takes on the narrow meaning of "choreographic patterns performed by actors." These include actions such as stepping left and right, pointing, spreading arms, opening the fan, and rhythmically stamping the feet. Nō choreography consists of sequences of such patterns performed in different combinations at different locations on the stage. It may be said that *kata* form the choreographic vocabulary of nō. Like other aspects of performance, such as music, melody, costumes, and masks, the entire repertory draws from the same definite gestural inventory. The most commonly performed movement patterns have names, such as *sashi* (point), or *sayū* (left–right step) that facilitate their transmission. In most cases, actors do not invent new *kata* even when creating the choreography of *shinsaku nō* (newly written plays).

Kata began to be written down in the late Muromachi period, when choreography books (*tsuke*) started to be created and handed down within groups of professionals (see Chapter 1, Nō as leisure). Even today it is common for practitioners to write down *kata* along with the text in a chant book (*utaibon*), thus creating a choreography book (*kata tsuke*). Movement instructions could be something like: *sashi*, *sumi yuki*, *sumi tori*, *ōgi kazashi*. These names make little sense until one learns the content. This sequence would translate to: point with the open fan in the right hand by tracing an arc from the waist, above the head, stopping at the height of the sternum (*sashi*), then keep this position while walking toward *sumi* (downstage right) starting from the right foot (*sumi yuki*), face the front of the stage by stepping back left–right (*sumi tori*), while at the same time extending the right hand, reversing the fan grip, and lifting it above the right shoulder (*ōgi kazashi*).

Assuming one understands the content of each *kata*, these are only general indications of *what* movement is to be performed. What choreography books lack are instructions on *how* to perform them. This is another example of "epistemic gap" in nō, where indeterminacy leaves room for individual interpretation by the performer, and thus affects not only the immediate contingency of the performance but also, importantly, the development of style. It may not be an exaggeration to say that it is the indeterminacy of the form that allows for a transformation of art that can still claim to be "true to its origins." This dynamic exists precisely because of the nature of corporeal transmission.

Movement in context

Building on the foundational work of Yokomichi Mario in 1987, nō scholars Monica Bethe and Karen Brazell have developed a useful analytical framework for nō movements.

Bethe and Brazell group movements into two main categories: "ground patterns" and "design patterns."[19] Ground patterns are more frequently executed and form the basis for most dance (*mai*) sections. In contrast, design patterns, less frequent and typically appearing in narrative dances (*shimai*), can be further subdivided into "abstract" and "mimetic."

Ground patterns include stepping forward or backward, circling the stage to the left or right, pointing and opening, zigzagging while pointing, and circling the fan above the head. These *kata* carry no intrinsic meaning, but they acquire significance when juxtaposed with text. A frequently performed ground pattern, *sashikomi hiraki* (or *shikake hiraki*, depending on the school), consists of stepping forward while pointing with the fan and stepping back while spreading both arms. When this movement is juxtaposed to text, as in the *kuse* section of *Atsumori* "we camped here at Ichi no tani," it appears as if Atsumori is pointing with the fan to indicate the place where his clan camped.[20] Certain ground patterns, for example foot stamps, may have multiple functions, such as marking the rhythm in instrumental dances (decorative function), express a strong emotion when combined with words in chant dances (highlight function), or indicating the end of a play (formal function). In sum, the function of this kind of *kata* depends heavily on context.

Design patterns are slightly more complex than ground patterns, occur less frequently, and are not as versatile. These *kata* are often used to emphasize narrative moments, especially through fan manipulation. Some design patterns bear a close resemblance to the object they represent; hence they are associated with the concept of *monomane* (imitation). For example, movements that imitate drawing a sword and slashing or shooting an arrow can be said to have an intrinsic meaning. Bringing one or both hands close to the eyes while leaning forward (*shiori*) is a stylization of the act of weeping and is often used to express grief (see Figure 9 left). Other design patterns have a less narrow correlation between their form and their meaning. For example, the "feather fan" (*hane ōgi*) sequence, in which the actor brings the open fan held in the left hand to rest on the right shoulder and sweeps the extended fan to the left, can symbolize a variety of things, such as the wind blowing or arrows falling from the sky. Finally, many actions that are considered *kata* do not have specific names and include mimetic gestures (such as scooping water or carrying heavy objects), object handling (sticks, halberds, etc.), or complex fan movement routines.

Kata are combined in more or less conventional ways. For instance, *kuse* sections typically begin upstage center with a closed fan, which is open halfway through in a section called *age ha*, followed by a left/right zigzag (*sayū*), arm circling (*uchikomi*), and arm spreading (*hiraki*). This customary sequence takes different meanings depending on the text to which it is associated. The second half of *Atsumori*, for which we provided a literary analysis in Chapter 2, is shown in Table 3.[21]

Although there is no strict correlation between the movement and the text, it is possible to associate the raising of the fan with the wind blowing downhill, while the left and right movements refer to the cold fields by the sea and the ships over which the plovers cry. The spreading of the arms shows the wide sleeves of the costume, one of which is then wrapped

TABLE 3 *Movement analysis of an excerpt from* Atsumori.

Text	Movements
While winds swept down upon us off the hills	Opens the fan, raises it above the head and to the right (ground *kata*)
The fields were bitterly cold. At the sea's edge	Five steps to the left, left foot stamp (ground *kata*)
our ships huddled close, while day and night / the plovers cried	Seven steps to the right, circles fan and points (ground *kata*)
and our own poor sleeves	Spreads arms (ground *kata*)
wilted in the spray that drenched the beach	Wraps the left sleeve around raised arm and kneels (design *kata*)

around the arm and raised while kneeling, in a variation of the "pillow fan," hinting at the clansmen resting on the beach (Figure 7 left), anticipating the line: "Together in the seafolk's huts we slept." Here the sleeve-wrapping design *kata* stands out at the end of a sequence of ground *kata*.

The final scene of a piece, or *kiri*, is its fastest and most dynamic part, following the *jo-ha-kyū* progression. These sections usually contain a large number of design *kata*. For example, in *Atsumori*'s *kiri*, the movements show how Naozane called him from behind and turned his horse to face Naozane. After exchanging a few blows, they grabbed each other and fell from the horse. Atsumori's beheading is depicted by the *shite* raising the open fan above his head and dropping the paper edge behind, a symbolic gesture also used in other plays to indicate that the character has been killed. When Atsumori pardons Naozane, he drops his sword and presses his palms together in prayer (a design *kata* known as *gasshō*).

When watching a nō performance without a working knowledge of both the text of the play and the dance customs, it may be difficult to understand the meaning of most of the movements. Dances appear as abstract, only occasionally punctuated by gestures that resemble actions from everyday life, such as striking with a sword, or holding the reins when riding a horse. This is due to the fact that movements generally do not aim to realistically imitate the corresponding part of the text to which they are associated. Therefore, *kata* should not be seen as directly correlating to specific textual elements. Rather, they are visual aids, supporting the viewers in their act of interpreting the connection between the text and the physical enactment.

Like any kind of performance, *kata* can be analyzed from multiple points of view.[22] One could focus on the sensory and physical experiences of movement in performance, delving into factors such as the actor's anatomy, together with the speed, rhythm, and proxemics of *kata* (phenomenological approach). Alternatively, one could analyze how meaning is constructed through a choreographic pattern (semiotic approach). Movements can be understood as being the visual representations of the meanings emerging from the lyrics. However, these are not solely determined by the script; rather, they materialize within the viewer's perception. Additionally, *kata* have a "formal value," that is a function within the structure of the choreography. For example, certain *kata* might serve to signal the beginning or end of a section.

Dance sequences

Movements in nō extend beyond simply illustrating the spoken words. Significant portions of a performance, including entrances, exits, and dance sequences, are performed together with instrumental music. These elements play a crucial role in nonverbal storytelling. The same choreography of an instrumental dance may be adapted to different plays.

Mai (e.g., *jo no mai*, *chū no mai*, *gaku*) are longer sequences performed to a distinct flute melody, while *hataraki* (e.g., *kakeri*, *inori*, *kirikumi*) are shorter and may emphasize action over musicality. *Mai* occur in the second half of a play, where they emphasize the emotional climax of the story. In some cases the character performs a dance within the narrative of the play. In *Atsumori*, the *shite* recounts how, on the night Naozane and the Minamoto soldiers approached the Taira camp, Atsumori and others were asked to dance and sing, and he played the flute. At this point in the nō, the *shite* performs the *chū no mai* "mid-tempo dance" (see Figure 7 right). Dances of this type are devoid of mimetic movement, and it is up to the audience to imagine Atsumori dancing elegantly to the music of the flute just moments before he meets his tragic end at the hands of Naozane (*waki*), who is now watching Atsumori's ghost (*shite*) reenact this scene.

FIGURE 6 Atsumori: *(left) Teshima Kōji as the grass cutter, (right) Yamada Isumi, Sōmyō Tadasuke, Yukawa Ryō as the fellow grass cutters in the first act of the play. Kongō nōgakudō, Kyoto. October 24, 2021. Photograph: Halca Uesugi.*

FIGURE 7 Atsumori: *(left and right) Teshima Kōji as Atsumori's ghost in the second act of the play. Kongō nōgakudō, Kyoto. October 24, 2021. Photograph: Halca Uesugi.*

FIGURE 8 Sumidagawa: *(left) Kongō Tatsunori as the mother, (right) Hōshō Kinya as the ferryman, Kobayashi Tsutomu as the traveler. Kongō nōgakudō, Kyoto. February 11, 2024. Photograph: Halca Uesugi.*

FIGURE 9 Sumidagawa: *(left) Kongō Tatsunori as the mother, Hōshō Kinya as the ferryman; (right) Kongō Tatsunori as the mother, Kongō Sennosuke as the child. Kongō nōgakudō, Kyoto. February 11, 2024. Photograph: Halca Uesugi.*

In other cases dance is used as a more abstract expression of the psychological state of a character. That is the case with the *kakeri* sequence, often performed in plays featuring crazed characters or ghosts of warriors, which is characterized by erratic shifts in tempo to express the *shite's* emotional condition. In *Sumidagawa*, shortly after her entrance, the mother performs a *kakeri*, expressing her state of agitation over her child's disappearance. Dance and music may be seen as taking over the narration, capturing emotions too profound for words alone.

The word "dance" is the closest translation of the Japanese word *mai*, a word coming from the verb *mawaru* (to move in a circle), which describes the way nō performers keep a low center of gravity and perform circling movements around the stage. This may have to do with the shape of the stage on which nō is performed, which used to be outdoors, in religious spaces such as temples and shrines, but also on temporary square platforms built on dry riverbeds.

Music and chant

The importance of the music of nō is immediately evident upon attending a performance. Musicians and chorus are not hidden but sit on stage in full view of the audience, at the back and to the left of the actors, almost as if they were embracing them. The presence and proximity of these different performers enhances the feeling of attending a form of collective narration, in which all members collaborate through constant communication, supporting and stimulating each other. This visibility of the musicians blends auditory and visual elements to engage the audience in one grand choreography. As previously mentioned in Chapter 1, the popularity of chant and music in nō theatre is such that many amateurs study these elements independently of the dance.[23]

Instruments

Nō music (*hayashi*) is characterized by the elemental rawness of its soundscape. The nō flute (*fue* or *nōkan*), originating from the *ryūteki* transverse flute of the *gagaku* court music tradition, incorporates a small bamboo tube (*nodo*) that alters the airflow. This modification produces a uniquely sharp and resonant sound. The flute plays in entrance sections and has a leading role in instrumental dances. It also embellishes parts of a chant section with melodies (*ashirai*) that do not follow the pitch or rhythm of the chant.

The shoulder drum and hip drum have the shape of an hourglass, with drumheads made of horsehide and held together by hemp ropes dyed bright vermilion. Although seemingly similar, they differ in construction, playing technique, and, of course, timbre. The shoulder drum (*kotsuzumi*, lit. "small drum") is played by holding it with the left hand over the right shoulder and striking it with the right hand in a vertical motion from below. Squeezing the ropes puts tension on the drumhead and alters the pitch. Shoulder drum players moisten the drumheads with breath or saliva during a performance to further control the tone. The hip drum (*ōtsuzumi*, lit. "big drum") is held with the left hand on the left hip and struck with the right hand that wears special protection, in a horizontal motion from right to left. Unlike the shoulder drum, the hip drum produces a very sharp sound and has a limited range of tones. The skin of the hip drum must also be dried over a brazier before each performance. Shoulder and hip drums work as a duo and are often said to represent the elements of water (*kotsuzumi*) and fire (*ōtsuzumi*), emphasizing their complementarity. The stick drum (*taiko*) only appears in a limited number of plays, mostly those featuring gods and demons. Larger than the other drums, and with heads made from cow hide, it is placed on a stand on the floor and played with sticks. Because it constantly plays both upbeats and downbeats, it creates a regular rhythm and marks transitions of dance sequences with tempo changes.

Instrumental music is performed in entrance sequences like *shidai* or *issei*, and dance (*mai*) sections including *chū no mai*, *gaku*, *kagura*, and *kakeri*. Despite being essentially the same combination of set drum and flute patterns, these sequences are performed across the repertory with a great number of adaptations. Without a conductor, the drummers use vocal calls (*kakegoe*) to highlight the interval between beats (*ma*). The intonation of the calls is also necessary for adapting a single pattern to various characters and moods. For instance, when an elderly character enters, the music is slow, with long, languid calls to highlight the extended intervals between beats. In contrast, a warrior's entrance is accompanied by quick, sharp shouts and fast-paced music. *Kakegoe* highlight the *ma* while also signposting the progression from one musical pattern to another, hence becoming an indispensable means of communication for the musicians.

Drums play preset eight-beat patterns strung together in long sequences. Like *kata* in dance, these patterns have names, and there are more or less conventional ways of combining them. A musical section consists of a fixed combination of patterns, often with an introduction, a middle section that may consist of repeating some patterns in a loop, and a conclusion. The flute also plays preset patterns, with some degree of improvisation depending on the section.

Rhythm

Nō employs two primary rhythmic correlations between melodic elements (chant, but also flute) and drumbeats. In the first, congruent rhythm (*hyōshi ai*), chant and drum rhythms are closely coordinated, beat by beat, using various techniques to synchronize the vocal and percussive elements. In the second, noncongruent rhythm (*hyōshi awazu*), the flute melody or chant syllables do not correspond directly to the beats. As a result, the melody and drumming progress in parallel but without being strictly matched, allowing each element to maintain its own rhythmic identity.

The noncongruent sections where the vocal chant is in free flow are particularly challenging. Here, the drummers dynamically adjust their timing to align with the chant. For example, while syllables and rhythm may not be synchronized, the drums match the ending of certain chant sentences. These adjustments, which include altering the number of pattern repetitions and combining elements of different patterns, exemplify the performers' skill and the impromptu quality of nō performance.

Different rhythm sections are strung together within a play, often moving from moments of "chaos" (non-congruent rhythm) and emotional climax as a character begins to evoke a story or recall a memory (e.g., *kuri* and *sashi*), to moments of "order" as the central narrative section (*kuse*) begins. Because nō music is characterized by a limited number of instruments and a finite repertory of rhythmical patterns, there is a risk of the music being repetitive and predictable. Musicians avoid this by skipping beats within the eight-beat system, and by emphasizing *jo-ha-kyū*. Variety is further influenced by the individual styles of the performers and the differences between the nō schools, and requires constant adaptation by the singers and instrumentalists during the performance.

Chant

All lines in a nō play are delivered through chant (*utai*). Actors are trained to project a powerful voice that resonates from the chest and abdomen, utilizing vibrato in the elongation of syllables. This technique is crucial in a performance style where actors wear masks and lack artificial amplification. Vocal styles differ among *shite* schools and roles; *shite* characters typically sing in a deeper, slower tone, whereas *tsure* roles are characterized by lighter, slightly higher-pitched singing. *Waki* performers may adopt a drier style that highlights the lyrics. Unlike kabuki, where male performers have a formalized, high-pitched way of producing the female voice, male actors will use their natural voice to portray women. What indicates the gender or age of a character are the pacing and modulation of pitch, but these may be hard to detect by the noninitiated. Finally, nō chant is based on relative pitch, set by the *shite* or by the chorus leader during the performance.

Chant can be divided into speech (*kotoba*), semi-melodic (*sashinori* or *sashi utai*), and melodic. *Kotoba* is a form of stylized speech, with each phrase characterized by an initial rise and subsequent fall. *Sashinori* is a semi-melodic style between speech and chant, sung at a fixed pitch, with embellishments added to the final syllables. When performed with instruments, *kotoba* and *sashinori* follow noncongruent rhythms. Melodic singing comes in two modes: *yowagin* (soft chant), which uses a five-tone system and creates melodies more familiar to the modern ear, or *tsuyogin* (strong chant), which features a unique melodic system with microtonal shifts and glissandi within a limited range of notes. Typically, a play will alternate between these different styles of vocal music. For example, a dialogue might begin as *kotoba*, change to *sashinori* as poetic imagery and dramatic tension increase, and continue as *yowagin* chant by the chorus. Interpretations of chant can vary widely between *shite* schools, with different distributions of speech, chant, and use of *yowagin* or *tsuyogin*.

For example, in the first half of *Atsumori*, when Naozane and Atsumori (in the form of a grass cutter) first meet, they converse in speech (*mondō*), to then switch to chant as Atsumori quotes a Chinese poem about bucolic poetry.[24] Through verse, *shite* and *waki* now have a shared semantic ground and their relationship has come closer. The two characters continue their dialogue by completing each other's line in semi-melodic style (*kakeai*, noncongruent), anticipating the melodic chorus (*ageuta*, congruent), singing "[all these pleasures] are pastimes not unworthy of those who care to seek out beauty."[25]

Congruent rhythm between singing and drumming occurs when syllables are matched to measure beats, and can be divided into three types: *hiranori*, *ōnori*, and *chūnori*. *Hiranori*, the most lyrical and widely used, matches twelve syllables to an eight-beat unit, typically accommodating verses with alternating lines of seven and five syllables. *Ōnori* is based on one syllable per beat, is usually played with *taiko*, emphasizes upbeats and downbeats, and creates a steady, pulsating rhythm. *Chūnori*, lively and suitable for depicting action scenes such as a battle, fits two syllables to each beat, maintaining a steady eight-beat unit. It is also called *shuranori* because it is often used to depict dynamic sequences in warrior plays (*shura nō*). These three modes are used in different parts of the piece to create different rhythmic effects.

Shōdan

It is part of the nature of drama to provide multiple layers of action, emotion, and meaning, all at the same time.[26] This also applies to nō, where segments of the performance text called *shōdan* (lit. "small *dan*") integrate information about different dimensions of performance, including lyrics (prose/verse, meter), music (melody/rhythm), and choreography. *Shōdan* structurally exemplify the intermedial nature of nō. It is impossible to consider text apart from music, or choreography apart from rhythm. The manipulation of costumes, the use of masks, and the relationship to stage properties are also integral parts of this multilayered text.

Shōdan are the building blocks of a play, and of its performance. Although virtually independent from each other, they are strung together in conventional ways, as in the aforementioned *kuri–sashi–kuse* sequence. Some of these *shōdan* already existed at the time of Zeami, who, for example, suggested editing the structure of a play to put the *kusemai* section in the foreground.[27] Today, too, when actors create new plays (*shinsaku nō*), they use *shōdan* to build the structure, adapting the content to the form. Scholar Yokomichi Mario's seminal work led to the contemporary, formal definition and categorization of *shōdan*. He identified three primary categories: those with chant (*utai-goto*), those with instrumental music (*hayashi-goto*), some of which are dance pieces, and those executed in silence (*shijima-goto*). We provide here a few examples, following the beginning of *Atsumori*.[28]

The play opens to *shidai*, a prelude to the entrance of the *waki*, played by the two hand drums with flute passages to noncongruent rhythm. *Shidai* is normally followed by a chant *shōdan* of the same name, usually sung by either the *waki* or the *shite*, that serves as a thematic introduction to the piece. Its meter is 7–5, 7–5, 7–4, and it is sung in congruent rhythm. In *Atsumori*, Renshō opens with the lines "The world is all a dream, and he who wakes, casting away from it, may yet know the real."[29] These lines hint at Renshō's realization that losing worldly attachment is the way to rid oneself of illusions. *Shidai* of this kind is always sung with the *waki* standing at *jōza* facing the pine at the back of the stage.

Renshō then turns to face the audience, preparing for *nanori*, a self-introduction section. The *nanori* is usually delivered at *jōza* (which is also known as *nanori-za*). Departing from the lyrical musicality of *shidai*, *nanori* is performed in speech, without music. Renshō then chants his travel song, which we previously identified as *michiyuki*. Technically, this song corresponds to a chant *shōdan* called *ageuta* (high-pitched song), based on poetic text (7–5 meter) to congruent rhythm. The last few lines of this segment are accompanied by a few steps to symbolize arrival. The travel song is customarily followed by the short *tsukizerifu*, a passage delivered as speech confirming the arrival at a destination, in this case, Ichinotani.

Once the *waki* has settled downstage left, the musicians perform another *shidai*, but they differentiate their execution in terms of pacing, intensity, and perhaps length. *Shidai* is based on looping drum patterns that can be repeated or cut. Atsumori and the other grass cutters enter the stage, stand facing each other, and sing: "The sweet music of the mower's flute [...] floats, windborne, far across the fields."[30] This *shidai*, too, provides poetic images hinting at the nature of the character and its story: in this case, Atsumori's flute, and how its sound can travel long distances. Although there is no direct reference to this, the *shidai* may remind us of how Renshō heard its sound when approaching the Taira camp or make us wonder if its sound reached the Capital, luring Renshō to Ichinotani.

We now fast-forward to the second half of the play. The *kuri* and *sashi* segments are both performed to noncongruent rhythm, with free verse sung in melismatic style. They serve the purpose of preparing for the main narration, but also create emotional tension through their unsteady beat and ornate chanting. The main narrative section is the *kuse*. As we already pointed out, *kuse* is derived from the *kusemai* narrative chant-dance tradition that predates nō. *Kuse* focuses exclusively on the *shite*, who may either be seated (*iguse*) or, as in the case of *Atsumori*, dancing. Here Atsumori describes the hardships his clan had to endure at Ichinotani. The *kuse* is sung in *hiranori* rhythm, either in *yowagin* or *tsuyogin* modes, and begins at a low pitch. The chorus sings most of the chant, with one or two single lines in the middle by the *shite*, after which the pitch is raised. Especially when *kuse* occurs in the second act, it is usually followed by a dance to instrumental music, in this case *chū no mai*, a mid-tempo dance, featuring the two hand drums, sometimes with the addition of the stick drum. This dance is typically performed by characters such as women or young men.

These are just some examples to demonstrate that we can use *shōdan* to analyze virtually any play. For example, *Sumidagawa* opens with *nanoribue* (solo flute entrance music), followed by the Ferryman's *nanori*. After that, the Traveler enters to *shidai* music, sings *shidai*, delivers *nanori*, travels with *ageuta* (*michiyuki*), and arrives with *tsukizerifu*. Knowledge of *shōdan* enables the analysis of not only the narrative structure but also the interweaving of multiple dimensions of performance.

Masks, costumes, fans

Nō masks (*omote*) and costumes (*shōzoku*) are the visual centerpiece of a nō performance, in striking contrast to the minimalist aesthetic of the nō stage. Some of the masks used in performances today date back to the Muromachi period, while contemporary replicas of ancient costumes, intricately crafted from silk and gold thread, are exceptionally lavish and costly. These elements make nō a visually stunning spectacle. Together with movement and chant, masks and costumes work together to shape the identity of the characters on stage. Each *shite* school follows established combinations of masks and costumes (*idetachi*) to portray traditional role-types such as the village woman, the old fisherman, the elegant warrior, the fierce demon, and so on.

It should be clarified, however, that there is no exact equivalence between mask/costume and character. The same type of item or combination can be used for different characters in multiple plays, with only a few items being exclusive to a single character. For example, Atsumori's appearance in the second act, corresponding to the role-type of the young Taira warrior, is very similar to that of Tsunemasa, another similar character who is the protagonist of a different play. Similarly, the mask-costume of the mother in *Sumidagawa* bears a resemblance to the "mother" role-type as the *shite* in *Miidera*. Rather than speaking of rules for mask and costume choice, it would be more appropriate to consider how conventions that allow for variations and exceptions have evolved organically over centuries, growing out of collective tradition.

Masks

Ancient nō masks, dating back to the Muromachi period, have been preserved within actor families, patron circles, and religious sites, and are still used on stage today. The longevity of masks underscores the deep reverence actors have for them. Masks are more than mere artifacts; they embody the cumulative experiences of thousands of performances, connecting generations of actors in a continuous thread of cultural heritage and artistic expression. During the

Muromachi period, various masks were created, some of which gained significant popularity and began to be widely copied. By the end of the sixteenth century, particularly prized masks were established as model masks (*honmen*), prompting the commission of copies (*utsushi*). During the Edo period, mask making became a lineage-based craft, with carvers often signing their work.[31] Although making a nō mask essentially means replicating an old one, the makers add their individual style in the carving and painting so that even two masks of the same type never look exactly the same. This tradition evolves in a balance between the transmission of original models and the innovation of style. In addition to canonical masks, carvers may also create new masks for *shinsaku nō* (see Figure 5).

Nō masks are carved from *hinoki* (Japanese cypress), chosen for its lightness and durability. The carving is done by hand with chisels of various sizes using paper molds (*katagami*) applied to different parts such as forehead, nose, or lips. Asymmetry is intentionally created between the two halves of the mask to give a natural, dynamic appearance that changes with the actor's movements. The back of the mask is carefully carved to enhance the resonance of the actor's voice. Painting includes a base of crushed white shell powder and animal glue, with mineral pigments for skin tones, features, and shading. Some masks features hair (often horsehair) or metal inserts for eyes or teeth. A brownish tint adds depth to different parts of the face, while aging techniques create a patina, to make a new mask resemble the ancient original that it is replicating. Finally, a lacquer-based varnish protects the inside from sweat and often bears the carver's signature.

In general, masks are used for all roles except those portraying a young or middle-aged male who is alive in the narrative present, such as the grass cutters in the first half of *Atsumori*. Performing a role unmasked, a practice referred to as *hitamen* or "direct face," dates back at least to the time of Zeami, who thought such roles to be particularly difficult.[32]

Zeami advised: "you should make no attempt to imitate the facial expression of that character but to maintain your own expression."[33] The conventions establishing the need for a character mask probably originated in the early development of nō, based on adult male actors who needed to wear masks to portray characters their natural appearance could not convey. Today, there are several professional female nō actors, but since performance conventions have been established with the male body as the standard reference, the same rules apply to both men and women. For example, female roles are performed by female actors with a mask, while *genzai nō*, in which all characters are alive in the present time, are usually performed unmasked, even if the gender of the character does not match that of the performer.

Nō masks generally represent a character type (old man, young woman, demon, etc.), although some are used exclusively for a single role (e.g., Shōjō, Shunkan, Yoroboshi, etc.). While the standard Japanese word for "mask" is *kamen* (temporary face), nō masks are referred to as *omote* (face), suggesting a quality of "truth" in the mask, as if it were an object of revelation of the character it embodies rather than of concealment of the actor who wears it. Nō masks cover the face but not the head of the actor, and are usually smaller than the face, leaving the chin visible. There is no unified opinion on why this tradition exists, but it may be to facilitate voice projection. Additionally, it could be for maintaining overall proportion with the costume, creating a sense of lightness at the top and weight at the bottom.

Nō masks are traditionally categorized into six types, aligning with the *gobandate* system (Figure 10). The "Okina masks," used solely in the ritual performance with the same name, consist of a white mask for the role of Okina, with round eyebrows and crescent-shaped eyes, and a black mask for the role of Sanbasō, symbolizing agricultural rituals with a more rustic appearance. Both are characterized by the detached jaw, connected with cords. "Old man masks" depict characters that transition from human to supernatural forms within a

FIGURE 10 *Nō masks. From top to bottom, from left to right: Okina, Kojō, Chūjō, Ko-omote, Hannya, Ōbeshimi. Courtesy of Miichi Yasuo.*

play. Kojō is marked by wrinkles, has a yellowish complexion, and white hair inserts complement the wig used for roles of this kind.

"Male masks" range from youthful to middle-aged appearances. Chūjō has a white complexion, plucked eyebrows, and a shade of red on the lips, indicating the elegant appearance of a member of the Taira clan. Jūroku (lit. "sixteen"), used in plays such as *Atsumori* or *Tsunemasa*, is a variation of the same kind of mask and displays even more youthful features (see Figure 7).

"Female masks" capture the essence of classical Japanese beauty, spanning various ages. They feature classic fashion traits such as parted hair and plucked eyebrows. The most well-known is Ko-omote, a young girl mask used for a variety of roles, from village woman to flower spirit. Like Jūroku, it is characterized by a white complexion, fuzzy eyebrows painted on the top of the forehead, and reddish lips, reproducing the makeup style of aristocrats. Fukai or Shakumi, used for roles of middle-aged women, are characterized by a contemplative downward gaze.[34] Shakumi, whose name translates to "slanted gaze," is shown in Figure 10. It is used by the Kongō school to portray characters of mothers or wives, such as the protagonist of *Sumidagawa*. This mask intricately captures the multifaceted emotional states of a woman in deep grief, perhaps over the loss of a child, which is emphasized by the swollen eyelids. Complementing this mask is a *kazura* wig, neatly parted in the middle and elegantly tied in a low ponytail at the back of the neck.

"Malevolent Spirit masks" are for characters transformed into evil spirits, with the Hannya mask being the most iconic (see Figure 9). It portrays the resentment of a woman who has been transformed into a demon, with eyes slanted by a frown and her mouth agape in an eerie grimace, displaying both rage and suffering. Features such as gold eyes and fangs enhance the supernatural aspect of this character, an effect that was sought after at times when performances were lit by candles or torchlight.

"Forceful Deity masks" encompass a broad spectrum of supernatural entities, from demons to gods, characterized by their imposing and varied designs. Ōbeshimi, used for *tengu* roles (a mythical creature endowed with great mystical power), is characterized by its clamped mouth, suggesting the compression of energy toward the inside, as opposed to Hannya, which projects it outside. The black line above the head, visible also in Chūjō, aligns with the hat worn in this kind of role (see Figure 10).

Masks in context

Nō masks severely restrict the actor's vision: men and women masks have only tiny eye openings that limit peripheral vision, while larger masks for supernatural characters allow for better vision and mobility, often allowing the actor to see through the nostrils. To navigate the stage, actors rely on structural elements such as the pillars, or the sonic proximity of musicians. The risk of falling from the stage is real. In addition to sight, actors use their feet to detect gaps between floorboards and transitions in the stage area, and sound to measure distances, especially from musicians behind them. Just like with the polished surface of the stage, it may be misleading to think of the mask as serving the purpose of the actor. On the contrary, masks can be thought of as having "agency" in that their materiality, not just the will of the performer, determines how they can be used.

Tilting the mask up and down allows for dramatic effects known as *kumoru* (to cloud) or *teru* (to brighten), where a slight adjustment in the actor's hip or chest angle, rather than the neck, changes the mask's expression from sorrow to joy. Masks of deities or demons, less suited to nuanced emotions, call for brisk side-to-side head movements (*kiru*) to emphasize the character's supernatural nature, with metallic eyes creating a dynamic effect when they catch the light during rapid movements. Actors must pay attention to the orientation of the mask, making sure it is held at the desired angle. The direction of the gaze of the mask is especially important. In *Sumidagawa*, as the mother sits on the boat listening to the boatman recount how the boy died and was buried on the other side of the river, the actor angles the mask downward, clouding it. This gesture leaves us to imagine the turmoil in her mind as she visualizes the boatman's story, gradually recognizing her own son in the tale. The mask also has the power to project images beyond the mask, rendering the invisible visible. When used properly, it allows the audience to see through the mask's eyes. As Atsumori dashes from the bridge to downstage center, gazing into the distance with a slight uplift of the mask, we see the Taira warships that have already left the shore and are far out to sea.

Costumes

Unlike masks, costumes from Zeami's time have not survived. What we know from historical sources is that patrons would donate valuable garments to favored actors, who would then repurpose these items for stage use. Such donations were a source of pride for the patrons, symbolizing their cultural standing and support for the arts.[35] In his writings, Zeami mentions several types of costumes, including *nōshi* (jacket) and *kariginu* (hunting robe), both of which were worn by aristocrats in everyday life.[36] In addition, his drawings also help us understand how at least some of the costumes were used.[37] In the "Notes on Dramatic Imitation" of his treatise *Fūshi kaden*, Zeami discusses the challenge actors face in portraying aristocrats, attributing this difficulty to the unfamiliarity of such roles, but also indicating that they "should, nevertheless, make every effort to research their language, and inquire into their demeanor."[38] From these documents it is possible to guess how important it was to Zeami and his contemporaries to produce a convincing imitation of characters. Yet Zeami advised: "don't imitate every last detail of even lower occupations. It would be unseemly to bring them before the eyes of high rank spectators."[39] Even today, lavish costumes are employed for characters of humble origins. For instance, a character depicting a peasant woman might be adorned in intricate brocade.

One of the most famous garments first worn by the nobility and later used in nō is the *karaori* (lit. "Chinese weave"), a type of small-sleeved brocade known for its rich overlapping patterns of flowers and other designs. In the late sixteenth century, costumes created specifically for nō performances began to appear, blending unique, stage-specific designs with the fashion of the day. As the style of nō costumes became more standardized in the early Edo period, costume started to incorporate luxurious elements such as thread made from *washi* paper coated with gold foil. During this period, the Tokugawa shogunate also imposed restrictions on luxury among the wider population, and the use of *karaori* was limited to the nobility and nō.

While masks last for centuries, nō costumes have a shorter lifespan, typically around a hundred years, due to wear and tear on the fabric. They are kept in shape by stitching with braided thread and thick needles, which can damage the material and in time, render it irreparable. As with masks, current costumes are often based on traditional models, but new designs may be produced for new *shinsaku nō*, such as the veil worn by Desdemona in *Osero* (see Figure 5).

Costumes in context

Like masks, costumes can be divided into different categories according to their shape. The upper garments are cut as a "T-shaped" kimono with box sleeves with small openings at the cuff (*kosode*) or as broad-sleeved jackets with open cuffs (*ōsode*). Pleated "divided skirts" (*ōkuchi* and *hangiri*) are also used in various roles. Costumes may have a plain or patterned weave, or be decorated with stenciling and embroidery. Various accessories such as sashes, wigs, headdresses, and hand-held objects complete the costume.

In the first half of *Atsumori*, *shite* and *tsure* appear as grass cutters. Their costumes suggest their humble origins (Figure 6). The inner garment is a *noshime*, or plain weave silk robe, used for the roles of low-ranking monks or commoners. It is draped straight with an open V over the chest (a style known as *kinagashi*), similar to the contemporary kimono. This costume is usually worn in combination with an outer garment. In *Atsumori*, *shite*, *tsure*, and *waki* wear a *mizugoromo*, a broad-sleeved robe with open sleeves worn as an outer "travel" or "work" coat. This is usually made of a plain weave fabric in a single color and is unlined, making it lightweight. The long sleeves can be shortened and kept together with stitches, symbolizing that the character is doing some kind of manual work. In the first half of the play, *shite* and *tsure* carry sticks with grasses attached to them, which are later discarded for the striped fans used for male roles. Although they wear the same type of costume combination, the prominence of the *shite* is emphasized by a slight variation in color or weave that adds interest to his figure.

In the second act, the ghost of Atsumori appears in his warrior robes (see Figure 7). He wears a small-sleeved brocade kimono used for male roles (*atsuita*). Given his young age, the *atsuita* may contain the color red, which is associated with youth in both male and female outfits. Over this, he wears a broad-sleeved robe of gossamer weave with open cuffs (*chōken*), worn primarily as an outer garment and used to dress male aristocrats and warrior-courtiers. The right sleeve of the *chōken* is pulled back and rolled up to symbolize a quiver and tucked into the belt to facilitate sword wielding. Under this, Atsumori wears wide white pleated trousers (*ōkuchi*) with rigid panels in the back to keep them in shape. *Ōkuchi* come in various styles and are worn by both male and female characters, generally expressing high social status. A wig of loose black horsehair (*kuro tare*) is used, topped by a lacquered hat (*nashiuchi ebōshi*), bent to the right, that is worn by Taira warriors.[40] In addition to the sword used in the final scene, he carries a "loser warrior" fan, with a painting of the sun setting in the waves.

Like masks, costumes influence the physical expressiveness of the actor. The straight *kinagashi* draping binds the legs so that only small steps can be taken. This in turn forces the actor to increase the number of steps taken when it is necessary to move faster—this may lead to unwanted wobbling, hence it requires advanced skills to be performed successfully.

Acrobatic movements are not only physically impossible, but can also expose the actor's white underwear, which is considered distasteful. The tight, "tube-like" *kinagashi* draping also draws the audience's attention to the feet, which naturally causes the actors to be even more precise with their steps. In contrast, *ōkuchi* allows for much larger strides and acrobatic movements such as jumping or falling to the ground, which are often used in battle scenes.

Finally, broad-sleeved robes such as *chōken* anatomically expand the actor's body, making simple gestures such as *hiraki* appear larger, and also call for movements that can only be performed with this type of costume, such as sleeve flipping and wrapping. The wide sleeves of the *chōken* are commonly used in dance sections, both for mimetic purposes and to punctuate the progress of an instrumental dance. A typical example is the passage in the *kuse* section of *Atsumori* where the *shite* wraps his left sleeve around his arm as the chorus sings "and our own poor sleeves / wilted in the spray that drenched the beach," a gesture that is linked both intertextually and intermedially to the poetic trope of sleeping on sleeves soaked in tears, a semantic reference to the desolation of the scene (see Chapter 2, Narration).

In *Sumidagawa*, the mother, a commoner, appears in travel garb. She wears a *surihaku*, a small-sleeved costume patterned with stenciled gold or silver foil, that is worn as women's undergarment. Although the *surihaku* is often seen only in the area round the neck, some ways of wearing it expose the right shoulder and arm, or the entire upper body. *Surihaku* often feature repeating design patterns such as waves or grass drenched in dew, which may be the case for *Sumidagawa*. On the lower part of her body, she wears a *nuihaku*—a kimono with gold or silver stenciling and embroidery, featuring water and leaf motifs—wrapped around her waist. Over all of this, she wears a *mizugoromo* similar to the one used in the first act of *Atsumori*. Although the same costume is used throughout the play, there are some changes to create the effect of "revelation" found in other pieces (see Chapter 2, Disguise and revelation).[41] The mother appears wearing a hat of interwoven reeds covered in black lacquer (*onna-gasa*) that partially hides the upper part of the mask, creating a somber, mysterious look (see Figure 8). This hat is then removed to reveal the mask in full. She also carries *sasa* (dwarf bamboo) branches, which are used in this type of play to symbolize madness.[42] In the last sequence, she uses a small metal bell and a mallet to recite the *nenbutsu* prayer.

Fans

The fan is a key element of traditional attire for all performers, except for a few characters like the mother in *Sumidagawa* who uses different props. Fans are decorated with auspicious motifs such as cranes, turtles, and pines, as well as Chinese deities and natural elements like flowers and birds. Warriors carry fans with designs like the setting sun in the waves, representing defeat, or the rising sun beneath pine trees, for victory. Fans not only enhance the performer's body, making gestures like pointing or sweeping more pronounced, but they can also "transform" into various objects such as swords or cups, depending on the action. The fan's transformative power extends to shaping the narrative. Like the mask, whose gaze materializes what the character sees, the fan points to invisible objects, from distant mountain peaks to a horde of enemy warriors, from the mercy of Buddha to the longing for a lost love. Additionally, fans serve a formal role in dance (*mai*), signaling transitions in the music by changes in how they are held, a practice possibly rooted in how performers used to improvise the adjustment of the progress of the dance (see Figure 7 right).[43]

Stage properties

The properties used in nō are called *tsukurimono*, which directly translates as "made-up object." Like its English translation, this word has a double meaning. It can refer to the "fictional," dimension of performance, but also to the physical, "handmade" nature of these objects. *Tsukurimono* are simple objects that are assembled before the performance and disassembled afterward, maintaining the principle of freshness and novelty, encapsulated in the expression *ichi-go ichi-e* that pervades nō. The portability of *tsukurimono* may have originated at a time when performers did not have permanent spaces but formed traveling troupes that had to quickly set up and dismantle a performance and move on to the next.

Most *tsukurimono* are wooden structures, often made of bamboo, sometimes covered with cloth to give them different shapes. They can represent buildings such as huts or houses, but also carts, boats, bells, and so on. The most common is a platform (*ichijōdai*), which is used to create a space separate from the rest of the stage, sometimes in combination with other props, to symbolize an elevated object, such as a mountain or a palace. The actor may be hidden inside the structure only to be revealed later, or they may enter the structure at the end of the first act instead of going backstage and changing appearance there. It may be said that *tsukurimono* function as a kind of "visual synecdoche," displaying only part of the object they represent (e.g., a roof for a palanquin, a bed for a bedroom). Although *tsukurimono* can add an element of realism by visually materializing an object that appears in the story and is otherwise only mentioned in the text, they are by no means exhaustive representations but serve only as visual aids to the audience's imagination.

Objects can be positioned in various areas of the stage: Large structures placed in front of the drummers are used to represent buildings, caves, or mounds; others may be set downstage center, to draw the attention of the audience. The semiotic versatility of *tsukurimono* can be seen in how the object representing the well in the play *Izutsu* or the *torii* in *Nonomiya* serve as both place markers and metaphors for the past in which the characters lived (Figure 11).[44] Often these objects are on stage from the beginning of the play, where they are gradually charged with the meanings evoked by the

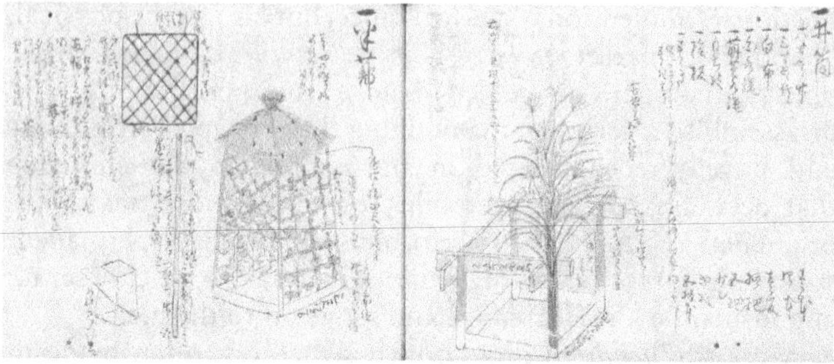

FIGURE 11 *Stage property drawing for the nō plays* Hashitomi *(left) and* Izutsu *(right).* Ōkura ryū tsukurimono hiroku*, by Yamamura Kyūzaemon, Edo period. Hōsei University Kōzan Collection.*

text, but also by the presence and gaze of the audience and the performers.

As the action of a play reaches its climax, there are often physical interactions between the *shite* and the *tsukurimono*. For example, the ghost of the woman in *Izutsu* pushes aside the pampas grass and stares at her image reflected in the fountain, or the ghost of Lady Rokujō in *Nonomiya* holds on to the *torii* pillar with her hand and steps out of it only to retract her foot, symbolizing the impossibility of releasing her attachment. In the fiction of the performance, the ominous presence of *Sumidagawa*'s mound, on stage since the beginning of the play, is not acknowledged by the characters until the last section, when the mother disembarks the boat. She approaches the mound and touches it while kneeling down. This structure is small enough to accommodate the child actor who, in a version of the play, chants the *nenbutsu* prayer from within it and then reveals his presence by emerging from it (see Figure 9 right). Interestingly, no stage props are used for the boat in this play, perhaps not to distract attention from the rest of the scene.

Conclusion

The authors of this book have had the privilege of discussing nō in various settings, including university courses, public lectures, and practical workshops, both in Japan and abroad. This experience has provided valuable insights into how different audiences perceive nō. Some individuals approach it with preconceived notions of inaccessibility, often expressing frustration over its archaic language. Others, less familiar with traditional Japanese culture, are often captivated by the enigmatic masks and movements, showing less concern about language barriers. For them, nō serves as an entry point into Japanese culture, offering a unique perspective for understanding its nuances.

Nō is a rich cultural repository that combines literature, history, philosophy, religion, ritual, theatre, song, music, and the crafts of costume, fan, and mask making. This multidimensional art form provides a comprehensive means of engaging with and exploring various facets of Japanese traditional culture, making it a valuable resource for anyone interested in delving into its complexities.

Since it became part of the standard education of the cultured class in the seventeenth century, a strong bond has formed between professionals, amateurs, and audiences, creating a tightly knit community of practitioners and enthusiasts. However, this interdependent system, essential to the continuation of the art, often maintains a structured hierarchy that preserves the established order but can inhibit dialogue and transformation. Numerous Japanese books and lecture series claim to teach the "correct" way to view nō, emphasizing how the understanding of rules enhances enjoyment. Even the act of reception may become a *kata*. While an understanding of the historical, literary, and philosophical contexts of the plays is crucial to deeper appreciation, nō has more to offer than mere adherence to rules.

Nō is fundamentally an exercise in imagination, requiring sensitivity and effort from its audience. Its narratives and presentation style are characterized by semantic and aesthetic gaps that the audience is invited to fill, making watching nō an act of connecting dots and interpreting hints provided by the performance. Avoiding realism in favor of abstraction and ambiguity, nō demands active engagement from its audience. Rather than offering instant gratification, it challenges the viewer to participate in the act of interpreting the performance.

Based on its long history as an official ceremonial performing art, nō is celebrated today as a representative art of Japan, further solidified by its UNESCO designation as an Intangible Cultural Heritage. Despite this, several issues have recently been raised, questioning its role in contemporary society. These include its lack of political engagement and its depiction of old-fashioned values, such as the role of women, or the relationship between lord and retainer, which are perpetuated in a social structure that does not invite discussion or debate.

Yet, nō is not only a cultural artifact but also a living tradition that continues to resonate with themes of human experience and identity. *Atsumori*, which explores the transience of life and the destructiveness of war, is a timeless reminder of the transformative power of understanding and compassion in the midst of conflict. Similarly, the poignant story of *Sumidagawa* portrays the universal struggle of a mother coping with the loss of her child. It also illustrates how sharing one's trauma and receiving support from the community can provide solace, highlighting the healing power of collective empathy through storytelling.

The potential of nō may also lie in the conceptual emptiness of its forms. *Kata*, essential for transmitting the art of nō can maintain their core while modifying their content. This adaptability allows performance conventions to evolve and to also be influenced by external sources, such as other performing arts. One of the great modern innovators of nō, Kanze Hisao, revitalized nō as a result of his exposure and collaboration with other forms of art both in Japan and abroad. Specialization in nō is crucial, as it enables performers to master the repertoire and reproduce it with minimal preparation. However, it may also be beneficial for actors to expand their horizons and draw inspiration from other artistic disciplines. Despite these advantages, the reality of their schedules—dominated by performances and teaching commitments—often restricts this exploration.

Japanese society is ageing, and nō in particular is grappling with significant economic challenges due to the gradual decline of its population. The numbers of professional performers, amateur practitioners, and supporters are steadily decreasing. This situation is further exacerbated by a predominantly one-way, top-down method of transmission. Without the influx of new individuals bringing fresh ideas, enthusiasm, and vigor, the art form risks becoming static. Young people, especially, are moving away from nō, as the prospect of a professional career in this field now seems increasingly difficult to envision. This trend highlights a critical need for revitalization and adaptation to ensure the survival and continued relevance of nō in contemporary society.

To address these issues, nō may need to proactively seek ways to engage with the world beyond its traditional boundaries and draw new inspiration for both its art and its business model. A progressive step for nō could involve encouraging the training of professional female performers and enhancing their work conditions by actively supporting their participation in high-level performances. This initiative would not only help diversify the talent pool but also promote gender equality within the traditionally male-dominated realm of nō.

Refreshing nō could allow it to continue to evolve as it has throughout its long history. This will naturally entail taking risks and reconceptualizing nō not just as an institutionalized art form, but as a dynamic artistic platform for innovation and global appreciation.

NOTES

Introduction

1 It should be noted that the terms *shite* and *waki* designate not only a role within the play but also the type of performer who specializes in it.

2 Fenollosa and Pound, *Certain Noble Plays of Japan*, 45.

3 The strong metanarrative element of nō, embodied in the *mugen* format, resonates with Marvin Carlson's description of all theatrical acts as "ghosting," or acts of conjuring the past. Carlson, *The Haunted Stage*, 2–3.

4 Zeami, *Performance Notes*, 59.

5 The website by Fujita, Rose, and Kapuściński, "Noh as Intermedia." explores intermediality in nō performance.

6 Féral, "Performance and Theatricality: The Subject Demystified," 173.

7 Here the word *kata* means "person."

8 Lave and Wenger, *Situated Learning*.

Chapter 1

1 The Taihō code was a set of legal and administrative reforms based on the legal system of Tang China.

2 Asukai, "Haru no miyamaji," 327–9.

3 An example of the legacy of this tradition is the Konparu school's performance variant of *Okina* known as *shushi-bashiri*.

4 Powerful aristocrats pressured their daughters to marry the emperor, ensuring that their grandchildren ascended to the throne at an early age. The maternal grandfather of the young emperor, serving as his guardian, could thus wield significant political power. While this practice was not exclusive to the Heian period, it was particularly favored by aristocrats during that time.

5 Nagashima, "Jōwa go nen kasuga sha rinjisai shidai."

6 Kan'ami is recognized as the founder of the current Kanze school.

7 De Poorter, "Zeami's Talks on Sarugaku," 85.

8 Cross-dressing is a feature shared with an earlier popular dance form of the time, called *shirabyōshi,* originating in the Heian period.

9 Zeami, *Performance Notes*, 364.

10 Pinnington, *A New History of Medieval Japanese Theatre*, 24–5.

11 Quinn, *Developing Zeami*, 7–8.

12 Yokoyama, "Zeami hakken: kindai nō gakurekishi ni okeru Yoshida Tōgo 'Zeami jūrokubushū' no igi ni tsuite."

13 Zeami, *Performance Notes*, 25–31.

14 Zeami, *Performance Notes*, 146–7.

15 Quinn, *Developing Zeami*, 7–9.

16 Zeami, *Performance Notes*, 47–52.

17 Japanese legends often describe the births of significant figures happening in extraordinary and urealistic ways that are beyond human understanding.

18 See Rath, *The Ethos of Noh: Actors and Their Art.*

19 De Poorter, "Zeami's Talks on Sarugaku," 91–2.

20 Amano, "Zeami to Saburō Motoshige – sono san."

21 Zeami, *Performance Notes*, 424–6.

22 Zeami, *Performance Notes*, 26–31.

23 Zeami, *Performance Notes*, 205.

24 See, for example, Takahashi, *Zenchiku nōgakuron no sekai.*

25 For research on Zenchiku's treatises, see, among others, Thornhill, *Six Circles, One Dewdrop*; Pinnington, *Traces in the Way*; Atkins, *Revealed Identity*.

26 The compound word tesarugaku includes the character *te*, which literally means "hand," but here means "skill."

27 Miyamoto, *Kamigata nōgakushi no kenkyū*.

28 Gosukōin, "Kanmon nikki ge," 63.

29 Moriya, *Kabuki no jidai*, 5: 207–10.

30 Kobayashi, *Jūhen ōninki*, 10: 758–61.

31 His last recorded performances date back to May 1596. See Amano, "Tokugawa Ieyasu to nō," 298–300.

32 Nishino and Hata, *Shinpan nō kyōgen jiten*, 316.

33 Sanada, *Meiryō kōhan*, 29.

34 Omote and Amano, *Nōgaku no rekishi*, 1: 110–11.

35 The nō play *Dōjōji* is based on a legend in which a woman transforms into a serpent and kills a monk she fell in love with, who is hiding inside a temple bell. The play's main character is a *shirabyōshi*, a female dancer who embodies the spirit of the serpent woman, dancing obsessively due to her attachment to the bell. The climax is marked by a special dance called *ranbyōshi* (lit. "crazy steps").

36 Omote and Amano, *Nōgaku no rekishi*, 1: 110–11.

37 These positions included corridor guards or *tokei no ma* guards, who were in charge of the room where a clock was kept, but during Tsunayoshi's era they were mainly used to promote nō actors into the samurai ranks.

38 Nishino and Hata, *Shinpan nō kyōgen jiten*, 322.

39 Yamamoto, *Bakumatsu kakyū bushi no kiroku*, 110–12.

40 Matsuoka, *Kanze Motoakira no sekai*.

41 Nihon Zuihitsu Taisei Henshūbu, *Okinagusa*, 3: 16.

42 Tanaka and Tanaka, "Shoji hitsuyō yoiku sou," 200–1.

43 Nishiyama, *Edo Culture*, 191.

44 Smith, "The Iemoto System"; Hsu, *Iemoto: The Heart of Japan*.

45 Sasaki, "Su-utai yoyo no ato"; Nishiyama, *Edo Culture*, 185; Rath, *The Ethos of Noh: Actors and Their Art*, 208.

46 Hōsei Daigaku Nōgaku Kenkyūsho, *Kōzan bunkō nōgaku shiryō kaidai jō*, 186.

47 Also see Nishiyama, *Edo Culture*, 192–7.

48 Groemer, "Elite Culture for Common Audiences."

49 Maruyama, "A Study on Tokugawa Shogunate's Management of Large Temporary Noh Theaters in Edo."

50 Hirano, "Kanjin nō kenbunroku."

51 Groemer, "Nō at the Crossroads."

52 Furukawa, "The Nō," 75–81.

53 The Kōka kanjin nō picture scroll, property of the Nogami Memorial Noh Theatre Research Institute of Hōsei University, is accessible online: https://nohken.ws.hosei.ac.jp/nohken_material/htmls/index/pages/cate5/kanjin-1.html.

54 Furukawa, "The Nō," 107–10.

55 Kagaya, "Nō Performances in Gaichi."

56 Fenollosa and Pound, *Certain Noble Plays of Japan*.

57 There is extensive research on modernism and nō. See, for example, Preston, *Learning to Kneel*; Houwen, *Ezra Pound's Japan*; Sheppard, *Revealing Masks*; Nishino, *Paul Claudel, Le Nô et La Synthèse Des Arts*; Leabhart, "Jacques Copeau, Etienne Decroux, and the 'Flower of Noh.'"

58 Smethurst and Smethurst, "Two New Nō Plays Written during World War II."

59 Satō, "Kindai ni okeru kaigai nihonjin kyoryūmin to nōgaku"; Kagaya, "Nō Performances in Gaichi."

60 Kanamori, *Joryū tanjō: nōgakushi Tsumura Kimiko no shōgai*.

61 Gillespie, "Interior Action: The Impact of Noh on Jean-Louis Barrault."

62 Geilhorn, "Between Self-Empowerment and Discrimination: Women in Nō Today"; Miyanishi, "The Potential of Women's Noh."

Chapter 2

1 For an updated list of nō translations available in foreign languages, see Watson, Michael. 2020. "Noh Translations: Noh Plays in Alphabetical Order of the Japanese Titles." Premodern Japanese Studies Website. www.meijigakuin.ac.jp/~pmjs /biblio/ noh-trans.html.

2 Zeami, *Performance Notes*, 285.

3 De Poorter, "Zeami's Talks on Sarugaku," 114.

4 There are several texts in the handwriting of nō actors from the late Muromachi period, but these were copies of plays made available to the patrons they tutored and contained plays by various authors.

5 The exact number of plays in the repertory varies. Some plays may be performed in one school but not in another. In addition, revived plays (*fukkyoku nō*) or newly written plays (*shinsaku nō*) may be added to the repertory of a school.

6 It is estimated that about 2,500 plays have been written since the Muromachi period, although a large number of these were not created for performance on stage, but only for chanting (see Chapter 1, *Utai* culture).

7 Zeami, *Performance Notes*, 105–8.

8 Historically, the classification was not rigidly defined, except for the first and second categories.

9 Zeami, *Performance Notes*, 77, 151–3.

10 Here *mono* means "piece." The words *mono* and nō are used interchangeably to designate a category.

11 Detailed scene-by-scene summaries of the plays have been published by the National Noh Theatre See Emmert, *The Guide to Noh of the National Noh Theatre*.

12 See Shimazaki, *God Noh*.

13 Here the word *waki* does not refer to the actor role.

14 McCullough, *Kokin Wakashū*, 3.

15 A concept known as *chisei sanbi* (praise of the reign).

16 Amano, *Zeami ga ita basho: nō taiseiki no nō to nōgakusha wo meguru kankyō*, 509–47; Takeuchi, "The Fusion of Narration and Character Voices in Noh Drama," 118.

17 See Shimazaki, *Battle Noh*, Shimazaki, *Warrior Ghost Plays from the Japanese Noh Theatre*; Oyler and Watson, *Like Clouds or Mists*.

18 Only three plays, *Tamura*, *Ebira*, and *Yashima*, are about warriors depicted as "winners." See Morris, *The Nobility of Failure*.

19 See Hare, *Zeami's Style*.

20 A small group of third-category plays (*Unrin'in*, *Oshio*, *Yugyō yanagi*, and *Saigyō zakura*) feature male *shite*. They are included in the third category because of their general atmosphere, and because they feature the *jo no mai* dance. For more information about third-category plays, see Shimazaki, *Woman Noh*.

21 Yoshimura, *Yōkyoku kōseihyō*, 53.

22 Nō scholar Shimazaki Chifumi has identified nine subgroups of this category. See Shimazaki, *Restless Spirits from Japanese Noh Plays of the Fourth Group*; Shimazaki, *Troubled Souls from Japanese Noh Plays of the Fourth Group*.

23 For a comprehensive guide on this play see Bethe and Emmert, 葵上—*Aoinoue*.

24 See Shimazaki and Comee, *Supernatural Beings from Japanese Noh Plays of the Fifth Group*.

25 Nakao, "'Mugen nō' to iu go kara nō no kindai juyōshi wo tadoru"; Tashiro, *Mugen Nō*.

26 Tyler, *Japanese Nō Dramas*, 45.

27 Pellecchia, "Introducing Genzai Nō."

28 Yokomichi, *Nō no kōzō to gihō*.

29 The two-part structure is referred to as *fukushiki mugen nō*. Exceptions are plays such as *Kiyotsune* and *Tsunemasa*, which contain the supernatural element typical of *mugen* plays but are presented in a single-act format (*tanshiki mugen nō*). See Yokomichi, Nishino, and Hata, *Nō no sakusha to sakuhin*, 3:31. Also see Hoff and Flindt, *The Life Structure of Noh*.

30 Zeami, *Performance Notes*, 151–2.

31 Zeami, *Performance Notes*, 152.

32 See Yokomichi, *Nō no kōzō to gihō*; Hoff and Flindt, *The Life Structure of Noh*; Yokomichi and Omote, *Yōkyokushū*.

33 Nogami, "The Monodramatic Principle of the Noh Theatre," 72. This may be associated with the notion of harmony (*wa*) in the nonconfrontational nature of Japanese society, but it is also a feature of the epic genre in general. Also see Suvin, "Revelation vs. Conflict."

34 An example of revelation in one-act *mugen nō* is *Tsunemasa*, centered on the musical funeral ceremony for Taira no Tsunemasa, a young *biwa* lute player killed in battle. Yet the appearance of Tsunemasa, first manifesting itself through the sound of his biwa, then appearing from the darkness, could be considered as a form of revelation.

35 De Poorter, "Zeami's Talks on Sarugaku," 111.

36 However, even in *genzai* plays like this, performance conventions may call for some change in costume to create interest on stage.

37 Tashiro, *Mugen nō*, 142–3.

38 They may be considered, borrowing J. L. Austin's terminology, to be "performative utterances" in that they are spoken words that perform an action. See Wallis and Shepherd, *Studying Plays*, 79; Austin, *How to Do Things with Words*, 6.

39 Jong, *Narratology and Classics*, 17–47.

40 For a study of narration and character voices in nō, see Takeuchi, "The Fusion of Narration and Character Voices in Noh Drama."

41 See Tokita, *Japanese Singers of Tales*.

42 Stern, *Philosophy and Theatre*, 4, 24.

43 See, among others, Salz, "Intercultural Theatre: Fortuitous Encounters"; Preston, *Learning to Kneel*.

44 Hoff, "Killing the Self: How the Narrator Acts."

45 In Japanese, verb tenses do not indicate the subject's person, and personal pronouns are often omitted, so translating the text into English often requires interpretation.

46 Amano, *Gendai nōgaku kōgi*, 219–23.

47 Tyler, *Japanese Nō Dramas*, 45.

48 An additional example of the arbitrariness of line attribution is how, in some plays, different schools (*ryūgi*) assign the same verse to different characters.

49 Smethurst, *Dramatic Representations of Filial Piety*, 6–17.

50 Tyler, *Japanese Nō Dramas*, 263.

51 For example, the phoneme *matsu* can be interpreted both as "pine tree" or "to wait."

52 Zeami, *Performance Notes*, 153.

53 Zeami, 153–4.

54 Shirane, *Japan and the Culture of the Four Seasons*.

55 Pellecchia, "Time in Noh Theatre Performance and Training."

56 Tyler, *Japanese Nō Dramas*, 257. Also see McCullough, *Kokin Wakashū*, 98–9, poem 411.

57 The story of the diver sisters Yukihira encounters in Suma later inspired the nō play *Matsukaze*.

58 Tyler, *Japanese Nō Dramas*, 46.

59 Indeed, in Zeami's time, nō texts were written solely in *kana*, while *kanji* were added at later stages.

Chapter 3

1 Shepherd and Wallis, *Drama/Theatre/Performance*, 193.

2 Iser, *The Act of Reading*, 181–2.

3 Ubersfeld, *Reading Theatre*, 73.

4 The northern nō stage at Nishi Honganji temple in Kyoto, built in 1581, is the world's oldest surviving permanent stage.

5 Miyamoto, "'Hokō' ni hajimari 'hokō' ni owaru."

6 The order of the five colors depends on the stylistic school.

7 De Poorter, "Zeami's Talks on Sarugaku," 85.

8 An example is the south stage of the Nishi Honganji temple in Kyoto.

9 Schechner, *Performance Studies An Introduction*, 145–9.

10 A similar action is depicted in myth of the Heavenly Cave, in which Uzume, the goddess of the performing arts, dances by stamping her feet on an upside-down bucket to lure the sun goddess out of a cave.

11 Pearson, "How Does Theatre Think Through Things," 122.

12 Okuhira and Hara, "Tabi ni tsuite."

13 See the illustration of the demon in Zeami, *Performance Notes*, 146.

14 Zeami, *Performance Notes*, 98.

15 Chow, "How Does the Trained Body Think?," 153.

16 Zeami, *Performance Notes*, 102–3, 131, 139–50.

17 For example, Yokomichi, Nishino, and Hata divide character types into four categories: ghosts and spirits (*reitai*), living beings (*genzaitai*), fantastical beings, such as demons and mythical animals (*fūryūtai*), and avatars (*keshintai*), referring to the appearance of the *shite* in the first half. Yokomichi, Nishino, and Hata, *Nō no sakusha to sakuhin*, 3: 20–1.

18 It is often mentioned how nō actors lean forward while standing but this description does not apply to all *shite* schools.

19 Yokomichi, *Nō no kōzō to gihō*; Bethe and Brazell, *Dance in the Noh Theater, Volume 1*.

20 Tyler, *Japanese Nō Dramas*, 46.

21 This analysis follows the conventions of the Kongō school.

22 See, among others, Fischer-Lichte, Mosse, and Arjomand, *The Routledge Introduction to Theatre and Performance Studies*, 49–70.

23 For research on nō music in English, see, among others, Tamba, *The Musical Structure of Nō*; Anno, *Piercing the Structure of Tradition*. For a detailed explanation of the nō music system with audiovisual samples of nō music, see Fujita, Rose, and Kapuściński, "Noh as Intermedia."

24 Atsumori references "sylvian lays" and "pastoral airs." Tyler, *Japanese Nō Dramas*, 40.

25 Tyler, *Japanese Nō Dramas*, 40–1.

26 Esslin, *An Anatomy of Drama*, 16–18.

27 Zeami, *Performance Notes*, 157.

28 We base our analysis on Royall Tyler's translation, but it should be noted that the performance tradition of different schools may differ.

29 Tyler, *Japanese Nō Dramas*, 38–9.

30 Tyler, *Japanese Nō Dramas*, 39.

31 For more information on nō masks, see, among others, Teele, *Nō / Kyōgen Masks and Performance*; Tanabe, "The Birth and Evolution of Noh Masks"; Pellecchia, "Masks in Traditional Asian Theatre – Japan."

32 Zeami, *Performance Notes*, 35.

33 Zeami, *Performance Notes*, 33.

34 The Kanze and Hōshō school use Fukai, while the Komparu, Kongō, and Kita schools use Shakumi for the same roles.

35 Takeda, "Fashionable Dress or Theatrical Costume," 76; Kawakami, "The Development of the Karaori as a Noh Costume," 107.

36 Zeami, *Performance Notes*, 32.

37 Zeami, *Performance Notes*, 140–9.

38 Zeami, *Performance Notes*, 31.

39 Zeami, *Performance Notes*, 31.

40 Minamoto warriors have their hat bent to the left.

41 In some plays, costume changes or modifications (*monogi*) may happen on stage. See Nakao, "Le corps du 'monogi'."

42 The origin of this custom is uncertain.

43 Also see Pellecchia, "The Fan of Noh Theatre."

44 The idea of semiotic versatility of objects in theatre is eloquently discussed in Pearson, "How Does Theatre Think through Things."

BIBLIOGRAPHY

Amano, Fumio. *Gendai nōgaku kōgi*. Osaka: Osaka University Press, 2004.

Amano, Fumio. "Tokugawa Ieyasu to nō." In *Tokugawa Ieyasu: sono seiji to bunka, geinō*, edited by Kasaya Kazuhiko, 286–305. Kyoto: Miyaobi shuppansha, 2016.

Amano, Fumio. *Zeami ga ita basho: nō taiseiki no nō to nōgakusha wo meguru kankyō*. Tokyo: Perikan sha, 2007.

Amano, Fumio. "Zeami to Saburō Motoshige – sono san." *Engekigaku ronsō* 11 (2010): 30–55.

Anno, Mariko. *Piercing the Structure of Tradition: Flute Performance, Continuity, and Freedom in the Music of Noh Drama*. Cornell East Asia Series 197. Ithaca, NY: Cornell University Press, 2020.

Asukai, Masa'ari. "Haru no miyamaji." In *Chūsei nikki kikōshū*, edited by Nagasaki Ken, translated by Tonomura Natsuko, 305–88. Shinpen Nihon koten bungaku zenshū 48. Tokyo: Shōgakkan, 1994.

Atkins, Paul S. *Revealed Identity: The Noh Plays of Komparu Zenchiku*. Michigan Monograph Series in Japanese Studies, no. 55. Ann Arbor: University of Michigan, 2006.

Austin, J. L. *How to Do Things with Words*. Edited by J. O. Urmson and Marina Sbisà. 2nd ed. The William James Lectures 1955. Cambridge, MA: Harvard University Press, 1975.

Bethe, Monica, and Karen Brazell. *Dance in the Noh Theater, Volume 1: Dance Analysis*. Cornell University East Asia Program, Ithaca, NY: Cornell University, 1982.

Bethe, Monica, and Richard Emmert. 葵上 – *Aoinoue*. Tokyo: National Noh Theatre, 1997.

Carlson, Marvin. *The Haunted Stage: The Theatre as Memory Machine*. Ann Arbor: University of Michigan Press, 2003.

Chow, Broderick D. V. "How Does the Trained Body Think?" In *Thinking through Theatre and Performance*, edited by Maaike Bleeker, Adrian Kear, Joe Kelleher, and Heike Roms, 145–57. London: Bloomsbury Methuen, 2019.

De Poorter, Erika. "Zeami's Talks on Sarugaku: An Annotated Translation of Sarugaku Dangi with an Introduction on Zeami Motokiyo." In *Zeami's Talks on Sarugaku*. Leiden: Brill, 2002.

Emmert, Richard. *The Guide to Noh of the National Noh Theatre: Play Summaries of the Traditional Repertory*. Tokyo: National Noh Theatre, Vol. 1 (A–G) 2012; Vol. 2 (H–Ki) 2013; Vol. 3 (Ko–M) 2014; Vol. 4 (N–Sc) 2015; Vol. 5 (Sh–Tok) 2016; Vol. 6 (Tom–Z) 2017.

Esslin, Martin. *An Anatomy of Drama*. New York: Hill and Wang, 1976.

Fenollosa, Ernest, and Ezra Pound. *Certain Noble Plays of Japan: From the Manuscripts of Ernest Fenollosa, Chosen and Finished by Ezra Pound, with an Introduction by William Butler Yeats*. Dundrum, Ireland: Cuala Press, 1916.

Féral, Josette. "Performance and Theatricality: The Subject Demystified." In *Mimesis, Masochism, & Mime: The Politics of Theatricality in Contemporary French Thought*, edited by Timothy Murray, 170–81. Theater-Theory/Text/Performance. Ann Arbor: University of Michigan Press, 1997.

Fischer-Lichte, Erika, Ramona Mosse, and Minou Arjomand. *The Routledge Introduction to Theatre and Performance Studies*. London; New York: Routledge, 2014.

Fujita, Takanori, François Rose, and Jarosław Kapuściński. "Noh as Intermedia." Noh as Intermedia, 2020. https://noh.stanford.edu/.

Fujiwara, Akihira. *Shin sarugakuki*, annotated by Kawaguchi Hisao. Tokyo: Heibonsha, 1983.

Furukawa, Hisashi. "The Nō." In *Japanese Music and Drama in the Meiji Era*, edited by Komiya Toyotaka, 75–117. Tokyo: Ōbunsha, 1956.

Geilhorn, Barbara. "Between Self-Empowerment and Discrimination: Women in Nō Today." In *Nō Theatre Transversal*, edited by Stanca Scholz-Cionca and Christopher Balme, 106–22. Munich: iudicium, 2008.

Gillespie, John K. "Interior Action: The Impact of Noh on Jean-Louis Barrault." *Comparative Drama* 16, no. 4 (1982): 325–44.

Gosukōin. "Kanmon nikki ge." In *Zoku gunsho ruijū hoi* 2, edited by Hanawa Hokinoichi, 2: 1–756. Tokyo: Zoku Gunsho Ruijū Kanseikai, 1930.

Groemer, Gerald. "Elite Culture for Common Audiences: Machiiri Nō and Kanjin Nō in the City of Edo." *Asian Theatre Journal* 15, no. 2 (1998): 230–52.

Groemer, Gerald. "Nō at the Crossroads: Commoner Performance during the Edo Period." *Asian Theatre Journal* 15, no. 1 (1998): 117–41.

Hare, Thomas Blenman. *Zeami's Style: The Noh Plays of Zeami Motokiyo*. Stanford, CA: Stanford University Press, 1986.

Hirano, Tomosada. "Kanjin nō kenbunroku" *Nogaku* 6, no. 1 (1908): 86–97.

Hoff, Frank. "Killing the Self: How the Narrator Acts." *Asian Theatre Journal* 2, no. 1 (1985): 1–27.

Hoff, Frank, and Willi Flindt. *The Life Structure of Noh _ An English Version of Yokomichi Mario's Analysis of the Structure of Noh*. Tokyo: Nōgaku Shorin, 1973.

Hōsei Daigaku Nōgaku Kenkyūsho. *Kōzan bunkō nōgaku shiryō kaidai Jō*. Nogami Kinen Hōsei Daigaku Nōgaku Kenkyūsho, 1990.

Houwen, Andrew. *Ezra Pound's Japan*. London: Bloomsbury, 2021.

Hsu, Francis. *Iemoto: The Heart of Japan*. Cambridge, MA: Schenkman, 1975.

Iser, Wolfgang. *The Act of Reading*. London: Routledge, 1978.

Jong, Irene J. F. de. *Narratology and Classics: A Practical Guide*. Oxford: Oxford University Press, 2014.

Kagaya, Shinko. "Nō Performances in Gaichi." *Asian Theatre Journal* 18, no. 2 (October 1, 2001): 257–69.

Kanamori, Atsuko. *Joryū tanjō: Nōgakushi Tsumura Kimiko no shōgai*. Tokyo: Hōsei Daigaku Shuppankyoku, 1994.

Kawakami, Shigeki. "The Development of the Karaori as a Noh Costume." In *Miracles and Mischief: Noh and Kyōgen Theater in Japan*, edited by Sharon Sadako Takeda, 101–23. Los Angeles: Los Angeles County Museum of Art, 2002.

Kobayashi, Masatoshi. *Jūhen ōninki*. Hōjō kudaiki, jūhen ōninki. Tokyo: Kokumin Bunko Kankōkai, 1912.

Lave, Jean, and Etienne Wenger. *Situated Learning: Legitimate Peripheral Participation*. Learning in Doing: Social, Cognitive, and Computational Perspectives. Cambridge; New York: Cambridge University Press, 1991.

Leabhart, Thomas. ""Jacques Copeau, Etienne Decroux, and the 'Flower of Noh.'" *New Theatre Quarterly* 20, no. 80 (2004): 315–30.

Maruyama, Nami. "A Study on Tokugawa Shogunate's Management of Large Temporary Noh Theaters in Edo." *Journal of Architecture and Planning (Transactions of AIJ)* 77, no. 674 (2012): 887–96.

Matsuoka, Shinpei, ed., *Kanze Motoakira no sekai*. Tokyo: Hinoki shoten, 2014.

McCullough, Helen Craig, trans. *Kokin Wakashū: The First Imperial Anthology of Japanese Poetry. With "Tosa nikki" and "Shinsen waka."* Stanford, CA: Stanford University Press, 1985.

Miyamoto, Keizō. "'Hokō' ni hajimari 'hokō' ni owaru: Hikaku engekiteki kanten kara mita nihon no dentō engeki no tokushitsu." *Nōgaku kenkyū: Journal of the Institute of Nogaku Studies* 45 (March 25, 2021): 25–40.

Miyamoto, Keizō. *Kamigata Nōgakushi No Kenkyū*. Osaka: Izumi Shoin, 2005.

Miyanishi, Naoko. "The Potential of Women's Noh." *Yūgū bunka kenkyū* 6 (October 2005): 2–21.

Moriya, Takeshi. *Kabuki no jidai*. Vol. 5. Kikan ronsō nihon bunka. Tokyo: Kadokawa shoten, 1976.

Morris, Ivan. *The Nobility of Failure: Tragic Heroes in the History of Japan*. Fukuoka: Kurodahan Press, 2013.

Nagashima, Fukutarō, ed. "Jōwa go nen Kasuga sha rinjisai shidai." *Nihon shomin bunka shiryō shūsei*, 2: 16–20. Tokyo: San'ichi Shobō, 1973.

Nakao, Kaoru. "Le corps du 'monogi': théâtralité du nô du point de vue du changement de personnalité." In *Théâtralité(s) orient–occident*, translated by Nakao Yukie and Jean-François Heimburger, 89–96. 11. Arles: Philippe Picquier, 2015.

Nakao, Kaoru. "'Mugen nō' to iu go kara nō no kindai juyōshi wo tadoru." In *Higashi ajia kotengeki no dentō to kindai*, edited by Mōri Mitsuya and Amano Fumio. Tokyo: Bensei, 2019.

Nihon Zuihitsu Taisei Henshūbu, ed. *Okinagusa*. 6 vols. Vol 3. Nihon zuihitsu taisei 3 Tokyo: Yoshikawa Kōbunkan, 2009.

Nishino, Ayako. *Paul Claudel, le nô et la synthèse des arts*. Paris: Classiques Garnier, 2013.

Nishino, Haruo, and Hata Hisashi, eds. *Shinpan nō kyōgen jiten*. Tokyo: Heibonsha, 2011.

Nishiyama, Matsunosuke. *Edo Culture: Daily Life and Diversions in Urban Japan, 1600–1868*, translated by Gerald Groemer. Honolulu: University of Hawai'i Press, 1997.

Nogami, Toyoichirō. "The Monodramatic Principle of the Noh Theatre," translated by Chieko Irie Mulhern. *The Journal of the Association of Teachers of Japanese* 16, no. 1 (April 1, 1981): 72–86.

Okuhira, Shizue, and Hara Masumi. "Tabi ni tsuite." *Kasei kenkyū* 14 (1982): 9–12.

Omote, Akira, and Amano Fumio. *Nōgaku no rekishi*. Edited by Yokomichi Mario, Koyama Hiroshi, and Omote Akira. 7 vols. Vol. 1. Iwanami kōza nō kyōgen. Tōkyō: Iwanami shoten, 1987.

Oyler, Elizabeth, and Michael Watson, eds. *Like Clouds or Mists: Studies and Translations of Nō Plays of the Genpei War*. Ithaca, NY: Cornell University Press, 2013.

Pearson, Mike. "How Does Theatre Think through Things." In *Thinking through Theatre and Performance*, edited by Maaike Bleeker, Adrian Kear, Joe Kelleher, and Heike Roms, 115–29. London: Bloomsbury Methuen, 2019.

Pellecchia, Diego. "Introducing Genzai Nō: Categorization and Conventions, with a Focus on Ataka and Mochizuki." *Mime Journal* 27, no. 1 (2021): 1–16.

Pellecchia, Diego. "Masks in Traditional Asian Theatre – Japan." In *Routledge Handbook of Asian Theatre*, edited by Siyuan Liu, 160–64. Routledge Handbooks. London: Routledge, 2016.

Pellecchia, Diego. "The Fan of Noh Theatre: Object of Encounter." *Platform* 3, no. 2 (2008): 33–46.

Pellecchia, Diego. "Time in Noh Theatre Performance and Training: Conversations with Udaka Tatsushige." In *Time and Performer Training*, 43–9. London: Routledge, 2019.

Pinnington, Noel. *A New History of Medieval Japanese Theatre*. Basingstoke: Palgrave, 2019.

Pinnington, Noel. *Traces in the Way: Michi and the Writings of Komparu Zenchiku*. Ithaca, NY: Cornell University Press, 2006.

Preston, Carrie J. *Learning to Kneel: Noh, Modernism, and Journeys in Teaching*. Modernist Latitudes. New York: Columbia University Press, 2016.

Quinn, Shelley Fenno. *Developing Zeami*. Honolulu: University of Hawai'i Press, 2005.

Rath, Eric. *The Ethos of Noh: Actors and Their Art*. Cambridge, MA: Harvard University Press, 2004.

Salz, Jonah. "Intercultural Theatre: Fortuitous Encounters." In *A History of Japanese Theatre*, edited by Jonah Salz, 513–28. Cambridge: Cambridge University Press, 2018.

Sanada, Masushige. *Meiryō kōhan*. Kokusho kankōkai sōsho. Tokyo: Kokusho Kankōkai, 45.

Sasaki, Haruyuki. "Su-utai yoyo no ato." In *Nihon shomin bunka shiryō shūsei*, edited by Nishino Haruo, 3:657–84. Tokyo: San'ichi Shobō, 1978.

Satō, Kazumichi. "Kindai ni okeru kaigai nihonjin kyoryūmin to nōgaku." *Nō to kyōgen*, no. 16 (June 2018): 70–89.

Schechner, Richard. *Performance Studies: An Introduction*. 4th ed. London: Routledge, 2020.

Shepherd, Simon, and Mick Wallis. *Drama/Theatre/Performance*. London: Routledge, 2004.

Sheppard, W. Anthony. *Revealing Masks: Exotic Influences and Ritualized Performance in Modernist Music Theater*. Oakland: University of California Press, 2001.

Shimazaki, Chifumi. *Battle Noh*. Cornell East Asia Series 91. Tokyo: Hinoki Shoten, 1987.

Shimazaki, Chifumi. *God Noh*. 1st ed. Tokyo: Hinoki Shoten, 1972.

Shimazaki, Chifumi. *Restless Spirits from Japanese Noh Plays of the Fourth Group*. Cornell East Asia Series. Ithaca, NY: Cornell University Press, 1995.

Shimazaki, Chifumi. *Troubled Souls from Japanese Noh Plays of the Fourth Group: Parallel Translations with Running Commentary*. Cornell East Asia Series. Ithaca, NY: Cornell University Press, 1998.

Shimazaki, Chifumi. *Warrior Ghost Plays from the Japanese Noh Theatre: Parallel Translations with Running Commentary*. Cornell East Asia Series. Ithaca, NY: Cornell University Press, 1993.

Shimazaki, Chifumi. *Woman Noh: In Parallel Translations with an Introduction and Running Commentaries*. 1st ed. Tokyo: Hinoki Shoten, 1976.

Shimazaki, Chifumi, and Stephen Comee, eds. *Supernatural Beings from Japanese Noh Plays of the Fifth Group: Parallel Translations with Running Commentary*. Cornell East Asia Series. Ithaca, NY: Cornell University Press, 2012.

Shirane, Haruo. *Japan and the Culture of the Four Seasons: Nature, Literature, and the Arts*. New York: Columbia University Press, 2012.

Smethurst, Mae. *Dramatic Representations of Filial Piety*. Cornell East Asia Series 97. Ithaca, NY: Cornell University Press, 1998.

Smethurst, Mae, and Richard Smethurst. "Two New Nō Plays Written during World War II." In *Nō Theatre Transversal*, edited by Stanca Scholz-Cionca and Christopher Balme, 31–7. Munich: iudicium, 2008.

Smith, Robert. "The Iemoto System." In *Learning in Likely Places: Varieties of Apprenticeship in Japan*, edited by John Singleton, 23–34. Cambridge; New York: Cambridge University Press, 1998.

Stern, Tom. *Philosophy and Theatre: An Introduction*. London: Routledge, 2014.

Suvin, Darko. "Revelation vs. Conflict: A Lesson from Nô Plays for a Comparative Dramaturgy." *Theatre Journal* 46, no. 4 (1994): 523–38.

Takahashi, Yūsuke. *Zenchiku nōgakuron no sekai*. Tokyo: Keiō Gijuku Daigaku Shuppankai, 2014.

Takeda, Sharon. "Fashionable Dress or Theatrical Costume: Textiles and the Evolution of Noh Robes." In *Miracles and Mischief: Noh and Kyōgen Theater in Japan*, edited by Sharon Sadako Takeda, 70–100. Los Angeles: Los Angeles County Museum of Art, 2002.

Takeuchi, Akiko. "The Fusion of Narration and Character Voices in Noh Drama: A Narratological Approach to Zeami's God Plays and Warrior Plays," edited by Sebastian Balmes. *BmE Special Issue – Narratological Perspectives on Premodern Japanese Literature*, no. 7 (July 31, 2020): 113–49.

Tamba, Akira. *The Musical Structure of Nō*. Tokyo: Tokai University Press, 1981.

Tanabe, Saburosuke. "The Birth and Evolution of Noh Masks." In *Miracles and Mischief: Noh and Kyōgen Theater in Japan*, edited by Sharon Sadako Takeda, 43–69. Los Angeles: Los Angeles County Museum of Art, 2002.

Tanaka, Chitako, and Tanaka Hatsuo, eds. "Shoji hitsuyō yoiku sou." In *Edoki 4: fujin yōsō hoka nanahen*, 4:127–203. Kaseigaku bunken shūsei zokuhen. Tokyo: Watanabe shoten, 1971.

Tashiro, Ken'ichirō. *Mugen nō*. Tokyo: Asahi shinbunsha, 1994.

Teele, Rebecca, ed. *Nō / Kyōgen Masks and Performance: Essays and Interviews*. Mime Journal 1984. Claremont, CA: Pomona College Theater Department for the Claremont Colleges, 1984.

Thornhill, Arthur H. *Six Circles, One Dewdrop: The Religio-Aesthetic World of Komparu Zenchiku*. Princeton, NJ: Princeton University Press, 1993.

Tokita, Alison. *Japanese Singers of Tales: Ten Centuries of Performed Narrative*. SOAS Musicology Series. Farnham; Burlington, VT: Ashgate, 2015.

Tyler, Royall. *Japanese Nō Dramas*. London: Penguin, 1992.

Ubersfeld, Anne. *Reading Theatre*, edited by Paul Perron and Patrick Debbèche, translated by Frank Collins. Toronto Studies in Semiotics. Toronto; Buffalo: University of Toronto Press, 1999.

Wallis, Mick, and Simon Shepherd. *Studying Plays*. 4th ed. London: Bloomsbury, 2018.

Yamamoto, Masahiro. *Bakumatsu kakyū bushi no kiroku*. Tokyo: Jiji tsūshinsha, 1985.

Yokomichi, Mario. *Nō no kōzō to gihō*, edited by Yokomichi Mario, Koyama Hiroshi, and Omote Akira. 7 vols. Vol. 4. Iwanami kōza nō kyōgen. Tokyo: Iwanami shoten, 1987.

Yokomichi, Mario, and Omote Akira, eds. *Yōkyokushū*. 2 vols. Nihon koten bungaku taikei, 40,41. Tokyo: Iwanami shoten, 1960.

Yokomichi, Mario, Nishino Haruo, and Hata Hisashi. *Nō no sakusha to sakuhin*, edited by Yokomichi Mario, Koyama Hiroshi, and Omote Akira. 7 vols. Vol. 3 Iwanami kōza nō kyōgen. Tokyo: Iwanami shoten, 1987.

Yokoyama, Tarō. "Zeami hakken: kindai nō gakurekishi ni okeru Yoshida Tōgo 'Zeami jūrokubushū' no igi ni tsuite." *Chōiki bunka kagaku kiyō*, no. 9 (2004): 19–45.

Yoshimura, Haruo. *Yōkyoku kōseihyō*. Tokyo: Hinoki Shoten, 2014.

Zeami, Motokiyo. *Performance Notes*, translated by Tom Hare. New York: Columbia University Press, 2008.

RECOMMENDED ONLINE RESOURCES

Websites on nō in English

Invitation to Nohgaku (Japan Arts Council) https://www2.ntj.jac.go.jp/unesco/noh/en/
JPARC.online https://jparc.online/nohgaku
Noh as Intermedia (Stanford University) https://noh.stanford.edu
The Nohgaku Performers' Association (Nōgaku Kyōkai) https://www.nohgaku.or.jp/en/the-noh.com

Museum websites with nō costume and mask collections

E-museum (National Institutes for Cultural Heritage) https://www.nich.go.jp/en/
Metropolitan Museum of Art https://www.metmuseum.org
Museum of Fine Arts Boston https://www.mfa.org
RISD (The Museum of Art, Rhode Island School of Design) https://risdmuseum.org
Tokyo National Museum https://www.tnm.jp

INDEX

This index aims to identify key concepts throughout the book to accommodate a range of readers, particularly those new to nō and non-Japanese speakers. Where possible, both English and Japanese terms have been included, with the entry being consolidated under the most common or most broadly encompassing term. Nō, as an integrated art (*sōgō geijutsu*) the elements of performance are interconnected, with text, movement, costumes, and music all playing a role at any given point. Consequently, terms related to these elements appear frequently in the detailed performance descriptions within the book. However, this index does not attempt to list every passing reference, as doing so would not be practical or helpful. Instead, page ranges are provided only where the term plays a prominent role in the discussion.